THE
POWER
— TO —
PERSEVERE

EK JASMINE

CLMPublishing

Contact the author at:
booksbyjasmine@gmail.com
Published by CLM Publishing.
Cayman Islands.
www.clmpublishing.com

ISBN 978-1-948074-19-3

This title is also available in eBook.

Printed in the United States of America.

If you can't fly, then run,
If you can't run, then walk,
If you can't walk, then crawl,
But whatever you do, you have to keep moving forward.

– Dr. Martin Luther King, Jr.

CONTENTS

1

MAKE A START

I have no authentic data to indicate how many of us endure successfully through our issues, but one point I am employing as evidence is Thomas Edison and his famous lightbulb *bust*: his ten thousand defeats. His progress after so many attempts showed me that determination is related to health training; you must stick it out to receive the results. No, I am not a health teacher.

I expect it would perplex a doctor or an educator, regardless of education, to see a baby walk or speak as it leaves the womb. An expert may crave the opportunity to study that newborn.

It's too extraordinary to overlook.

Likewise, it may shock you if you have not been practicing your enduring strengths, and then *voila!*

I do not think that as you commence to or complete reading this book – or any other book on determination – that you will metamorphose into a fearless perseverer.

Everything you try requires time to produce results.

Your power to persevere must develop its own energy to keep you moving; this comes from within you.

Take, for instance, the way a car works when it hasn't been in use for a period. We jump into it, turn the key, and, most of the time, put it into drive and go on our way.

For an automobile to be efficient in its proper usage, and if it has been sitting for a while overnight, it needs to be idled for a moment to warm up. This supports the engine to power up the rest of the car. Letting it get heated up allows the machine to work better.

So, too, in life, give yourself that fragment of time to "warm up," to wait it out so your journey can be more fulfilling as you progress.

The same can be said concerning activating your power to persevere or endure. If you have not been persevering well, give yourself time to get that thought whipped back into shape. You can warm up with motivations from others until you discover your own tempo.

Follow these basic steps:

- Commence by taking authority of your life; you know your own pace.
- Put the work into your improvement; if you are not working at it, don't expect good results.
- Work your way from a crawl to a stand-up-and-walk stage; breathe, breathe, and breathe.

When a car is started up after a gap since the last time it was driven, it may give off a *putter-putter* noise depending on the engine or the year of the car; some say *sputter*. As the heat of the engine increases throughout the pistons and plugs and the rest of running mechanisms, you will hear a quieter *purr* telling you it's ready to go.

You can get going, but you must start at the point of a beginner. You'll get to standing on your own power soon enough. For now – just warm up.

Whether you are a newly born-again Christian or a junior person just starting out at a new school or a new job, you may wobble a few times before you get it together. Give yourself the chance to experience the process. Keep in mind that even trained hikers or joggers stumble.

If the illustration of the car didn't do it for you, let's look at a toddler learning unfamiliar things.

Depending on the age of the toddler, three months or more, he may want to show he is clutching objects and may start showing his ability. He wants to do things for himself, such as rolling from his side to his back or from his back to his belly. Sometimes he holds on to whatever feeding device is in his mouth. Other times, if you put him in one corner of the crib or the bed, you will find him at the other side.

Soon you can't leave that kid alone on a bed or in a feeding chair as he will look for ways to get from lying or sitting to crawling and standing. Before long, that's not enough for him. He will check out his surroundings and will want to walk as he sees the surrounding people are doing it. He'll wobble around and take a few steps, trying to stand and walk in his own strength.

Sometimes the child may hold on to whatever is within his reach, a chair, a pet, or his parents' legs, until he finds the confidence to stand and step off on his own. As we cheer him on, the quicker his steps get, and soon his walking steps make him look like he's running.

As his body develops, he tries out more things.

You may start to notice he observes things to sidestep so he doesn't crash into the counter or the dinner table. He no longer sits *under* a chair because he is getting more intelligent.

He watches and tries to pattern what he sees. Day by day, if he persists, he will get better. He never and should not stop investigating his surroundings.

Soon that child, who, a few months ago, could not stand on his own, now wants to run around the house and the yard, showing off his independence.

That is the place those who are learning to persevere should get. We should take our time getting from starting, or as someone without power, to the warmed-up and charged-up stage.

We should begin by training our minds, hands, and legs to work in unison to keep us balanced.

When a boxer is training, you may notice that he combines several movements to hone his skills. He runs, skips, jumps, lifts weight, pulls weights, and throws punches at something, such as a bag, or shadowboxes with his trainer. He does everything to improve his chances of winning. His training comprises movements. He keeps moving. Standing still in a boxing ring is a sure way to get knocked out.

A boxer must use his mind, hands, and feet in a unified rhythm to stay in a championship mood. That method should teach us.

As you search for more persevering power, try to pattern one of the two examples mentioned: a child learning or a boxer training.

And before you think children cannot teach you anything, remember that even the Bible gives them high praise: "…**except ye be** converted, and become **as little children**…" (Matthew 18:3, emphasis added)."

Learning and development help us to move from one stage to another.

As you learn to persevere, know this: you cannot stay in the same place. Perseverance involves movement. "No form of matter is permanent. Change goes on everywhere, at every instant, by physical laws in the physical body and by astral and mental laws in our invisible bodies[1]."

A baby does not stay an infant. There is growth from a toddler to preteen, then on to a teen, and finally an adult. In every stage of that growth, he must adapt and create a fresh path to walk. What was okay at the toddler stage will not help him or be acceptable at the preteen or teen stage. The same goes for when he becomes an adult.

Newspaper editor and teacher, L. W. Rogers says, "We are not the same being, physically, mentally, or spiritually, any two days in succession. The very soul itself is subject to this law of change." But, one trait we should carry on through to adulthood and the rest of our life is integrity; that must never change.

In working on your persevering skills, it is best to start off honestly. If you are depressed or in a low state, be willing to let others know you need help. Help is available, but if you don't let anyone know you need it, and what you need, how can you get it?

A baby, when he wants attention or to be picked up, stretches his hands in the air. He may even cry out or roll around on the floor to get attention. I am not suggesting you do that. But do something. Even a baby has it figured out.

How did he learn any of those things? Maybe he learned them over time. Maybe he stretches his hands up because that's the way

---

[1] Self-Development and the Way to Power

you have lifted him before. Maybe he finds he likes how you come rushing to his rescue when he cries or when he lifts his hands up. Who knows? But my best *maybe* is that he activated from within.

As you look to grow in perseverance, think about this idea: "There are certain well-established facts about the laws of growth that we should not overlook when seeking the way forward. *Nothing whatever can grow without use, without activity. Inaction causes atrophy* [waste]" (L.W. Rogers, emphasis added). We are growing in body. Maybe we need to consider that we are or should also grow in mind. Many of the things we learned at four years old, we are not using now; however, our minds will recall and incorporate that information if we require it.

We all have abilities far beyond what we use and what we think. We have minds capable of building spacecraft to take us to the moon or satellites to see far into the galaxies. However, some of us have yet to tap into our minds to produce the success we want. The same mental faculty that came up with the idea of lemonade designed spaceships.

The ability to move from an infant stage to the adult stage, not only in body, but in the mind and spirit, is available to all; *it is a journey that we must make to get to that phenomenal* power. However, it must be something that we desire and will persevere to get. I believe that nature never gives life where it is useless, where it cannot or will not be used; this is the law of economy. If you don't persevere to a deeper mindset, you are causing degeneration of the mind.

Exercise increases the strength of your muscles and the full power of the body. To increase in strength, we must use our muscles. Likewise, "The only way to make the brain keen and powerful is to exercise it by original thinking."[2] If we want the *push* in our life, we need to activate our extraordinary ability and feed the mind to continue to grow. Start by working on strengthening your cognitive ability. The energy you need to survive a test comes from your spirit, but if your mind and spirit are not actively involved and connected, your body will not perform to get excellent results.

---

[2] L.W. (Louise William) Rogers

If we haven't invited our minds to the meeting of body and spirit, or vice versa, we are hurting our growth. Put your mind to work for you. Your intellect can handle more if you give it more to handle.

You may have been limiting yourself to what you think is acceptable or based on what people will say. Maybe it's time to get past that preteen peer-pressure stage. You don't need approval from anyone. Push on to your goal. Gather your thoughts to work in oneness with your action.

Depending on your age, that infant body may be well behind you, so lift your mind to another level. You don't get a pass as an infant would when behaving out of character. Connect with yourself. Praying helps you to connect, so add it to your daily routine.

L. W. Rogers says, "...apathy, inaction, idleness, uselessness, is the road to degeneration. Aspiration and activity mean growth, development and power."[3] I implore you to get a grip on what is going on in your body and your mind. Walk with full awareness that you can do this. If you have made it to this line, don't turn back now, and might I add, don't put this book down either. It is here to encourage you along your journey, to get to that point where you can walk on adult legs. Choose perseverance.

It is time to realize that: "The Universe is a training school for evolving intelligence—a vast gymnasium for the development of moral fiber. We become clever by playing at the game of life. We match our courage against its adversities and gain fearlessness. We try our optimism against its disappointments and learn cheerfulness. We put our patience against its failures and gain persistence."[4]

No man can avoid life, so choose how you live and enjoy it as you do.

Keep turning these pages if you are ready to become a persevering *specialist.*

Small steps add up to complete big journeys.[5]

---

[3] L.W. Rogers
[4] L.W. Rogers
[5] Matshona Dhliwayo

2

CHOOSE

I imagine by now you have tried to move. To get started. As you try to move from struggling to persevering, there is something you need to keep handy and use as often as needed: you possess exceptional abilities as a child of the King, so when you need help, ask boldly.

Nothing is too good for you. It is your Father's pleasure to give you the best. And unlike your earthly father, whom you might need to take care of when he gets older, God takes care of us throughout life, and He has also made provision for the afterlife. You should lack nothing.

If you have a need, ask with determination and persistence. If you find you are hesitating to ask, find out what is causing that hesitation. What would help you to not hesitate?

If you can believe God for the money to pay your rent, you can trust Him for your own home. For most of us, we ask God for the small stuff, bus or cab fare or food for today instead of car or groceries for the month. We ask Him to cure us of the common cold or flu, but not cancer. Our persevering *rhythm* seems to shut down at the very thought of the larger stuff. We get anxious and sometimes downright refuse to ask for what we want. We have the determination to go a mile, but we don't want to build up the stamina to go two or three miles.

Stick it out; *don't give up* until you have the success you desire.

There's a story in the Bible where Jesus heals two blind men. These men must have been hanging out near where Jesus raised the little girl from the dead. Everyone around her thought she was dead, but Jesus told them, "She wasn't dead but sleeping" (Matthew 9:24–25). Sometimes you and your situation are doing a lot better than you think!

Anyway, the blind men seem to have had a mission to accomplish, so they followed Jesus. I like to think they *heard* how the woman with the issue of blood persevered to touch the hem of Jesus's garment and may have *felt* the breakthrough method of faith, coupled with perseverance, for their touch. The Bible says, "And as Jesus passed on from there [the house with the child], two blind men followed him, crying aloud, 'Have mercy on us, Son of David'" (Matthew 9:27, ESV). Note, they didn't sit in the state they were in. Neither did they think, "We are blind, so Jesus will automatically heal us." No, not so. They used active faith. Not only did they follow Jesus, but they *cried unto Him*.

I can't emphasize this enough: when you need something, it is best to let it be known. Your thoughts can't be read just by being present. Only God can read your thoughts. Be clear and ask.

There is another story that is an outstanding example of what happens (or does not happen) when you don't ask for what you want. The story is about a man who came to borrow his neighbor's donkey.

The story states that the man spent some time talking about things with the neighbor, maybe about the weather, "remember when," or this and that. While they were talking, another man came on the scene and said, "Good day, Mr. X. May I borrow your donkey?" The owner of the donkey said, "Yes," and gave the donkey to the man. When the second man left with the donkey, the first man said, "I came to borrow the donkey."

How sad.

He didn't get the donkey because he spent his time *beating around the bush*. He left off the actual reason he was there. He wasted his opportunity with unnecessary conversation. And as the owner of the donkey couldn't read minds, he didn't know.

Ask and you will get it. Ask with confidence.

Maybe the first man thought he would lead into his request or that *it would be respectful* to talk to the man first before he asked for what he wanted. Maybe he was waiting for the *right opportunity*. He lost out because he used the wrong approach. *The right opportunity was when he first got there* and the donkey was available. He failed to be direct, so his journey will be harder.

Learn to recognize opportunities and act on them. You may not get another chance.

Whatever is lacking, ask for it, believe that you will get it, and give thanks.

The second man who asked for the donkey received a *yes* because he had a need and he didn't hesitate to ask. And when he received, he continued on his journey.

In the same way, the two blind men lacked sight. They *heard* what Jesus could do, and they set their attention on getting their miracle. They followed Jesus, even into a house. The Bible says, *"When he entered the house, the blind men came to him"* (v. 28). They went where Jesus went.

Never worry where the answer or substance is coming from; it will come. Never worry where you should go to get the answer. Once you ask, trust and have an open heart to receive.

The blind men *asked* Jesus to have mercy on them. They *followed* Him and *cried*. They persevered until Jesus said to them, *"Do you believe that I can do this?"* (v. 28) After all they had done to be where Jesus was, they still had to have the faith to receive the gift of healing. They answered, "Yes, Lord." Their *yes faith* got them an action from Jesus, who then *"touched their eyes, saying, 'According to your faith be it done to you'"* (v. 29, emphasis added).

You have the choice; it just depends on how far you will go for your breakthrough.

Humans are the only creatures that have the right to choose; everything else works along with nature as nature plans. You have the ability to overcome, to choose, to decide for yourself where you want your life to go. Whether you are a junior person in school or an adult in the working field or unemployed, we all have access to the power to persevere. It's that inner push to follow Jesus until you get your healing or whatever you desire from Him. It's that inner push to get to the inner strength that causes you to press through a crowd to get what you want. In a desert, it's that instinct to search until you find water. It's that *push* that gets you out of a gloomy tunnel to get to the light. It is that drive that causes you to seek shelter at the onset of or during a storm. I like to think no one gives up when he knows the result will be in his favor.

We pray when we can't find the answer, but we should pray even when we know the answer. You should still persevere even when you don't know what the outcome will be.

Sometimes it's when things are at their worst that a result presents itself.

Imagine two *blind men* walking, *following* Jesus. There was nothing to help them. They might have faltered or bumped into some obstacles, but they pushed on. When you have exhausted yourself trying, it's good to wait for a while. They were standing by the wayside when Jesus passed.

Wait. A prize is coming; just make it to the finish line.

A champion knows that only at the finish line will he get the prize, so though his muscles tighten and his entire body aches, he digs deeper to find extra energy. And even if your body feels like it can't go any further, there is that last bit of energy that kicks in to help you make it to the finish line. That energy only kicks in when you think you can't go on any further. Once you push past the give-in feeling, your reserved energy will take over the race for you. It is said that "the worse things get, the closer you are to succeeding." (Author unknown.) This has happened for me.

So, go all out to make it to the finish line.

Our Maker has *fitted* us with everything needed for life, including a will to go on. This comes from within us. God knows the end from the beginning. Every area of our lives was recorded before we got here. There are gifts available for us, but the problem is that some of us don't know we have them. Some refuse to extend themselves, and some just can't be bothered.

The blind men were destined for their healing that day; healing is a promised gift. Healing is the children's bread; hence, when Jesus asked the blind men, "Do you believe I can do this?" their "yes" was all it took to make Him touch them. "Yes. We know you can."

What if they had said, "I don't know," or, "I heard so." Maybe Jesus would have still healed them due to their willingness to follow Him. Who knows? Jesus has a plan for every situation; nothing can thwart His purpose. But what if they didn't continue? We can almost say they wouldn't have received their sight. They had to get close enough to Him so He could *touch* them. Jesus *spoke* some miracles, and some, He did with *physical touch*.

Sometimes we cannot get our gifts because we are uninformed. Other times, we feel inadequate or undeserving. It is like failing to go to the bank to collect a preapproved credit card or a check for a loan. The loan may be one hundred percent financed, but we think we are not *worthy* of receiving such a gift. I think some of us need some serious deprogramming of the mind.

When we were younger, we used to come running when our parents called us, but when they said, "Can't you walk?" we stopped running. Then, as we got older and walked slower, when our parents called, they would then say we should move faster!

"Stop running" but "come quicker."

Sound familiar?

Maybe we are the way we are, good or not so good, because of how we were taught.

Growing up, family and friends taught me to not look at other people's stuff or go into a store if I was not buying anything, because that is *red-eye* – begrudging others. It was even worse if the store sold expensive stuff. "You must not go in, because you can't afford it." I heard that so many times that I got scared and spent most of my adult life away from such *expensive stores,* as I concluded they were out of my reach. I discovered that it is okay to go into the shops even if they are *expensive*. It's okay to get familiar with the things I desire; I should feel good about expecting a marvelous house, or pleasing things to put in it. I should touch the superb stuff, get familiar.

There is a Scripture that says, "If a man desires [what is in] the office of a bishop, he desires a good thing" (1 Timothy 3:1, emphasis added). It's okay to desire magnificent gifts. Hallelujah!

It's time to rejoice. We, too, can take from the table the good stuff *(the good china)*.

Walk and claim your preapproved gift. God's divine power has "Granted to us all things that pertain to life and godliness" (2 Peter 1:3. ESV). "Everything you need to meet all the demands of life you already have, but the problem is, if you don't know you have it then you don't know where to go get it."[6] Some of us are still living on the outside when God, our Creator, has given us the keys to the kingdom; it's ours.

This reminds me of a story I heard Dr. Tony Evans once tell about the renowned publisher Randolph Hearst. It is said that Hearst was an avid art collector and there was one painting he wanted, so he sent his staff all over the world in search of it. They came back empty-handed. One day, someone cleaned out Hearst's basement and found the painting. He already owned it, yet he'd spent thousands of dollars searching for it. Hearst had inherited an enormous publishing company from his father, and he increased that company financially several times over, so he might not have been put out by searching for the painting. But the problem is, he sought after something he already owned.

The same can be said for many of us. We search for wealth and other stuff, when the Creator of the universe gave it all to us; all we need is to seek Him first.

As money is an issue for some of us, we cannot afford to lose time and money searching for what's already ours. Be encouraged to choose when an opportunity presents itself. Block all thoughts that are not beneficial to your growth or health.

I heard a speaker once say, "When thoughts of lack come to mind or the question of where money is coming from, banish it with these words: 'From wherever it is right now.'"[7] It's a knowledge I attained, and I try to keep these words in my mind and incorporate them in my day as much as possible. Those thoughts are serving me well. I have access to all the wonderful things pertaining to life.

---

[6] Dr. Tony Evans
[7] Dr. Joseph Murphy

Even Hearst's money came from where the painting was: his own publishing company and inheritance. Don't worry if you don't have a business; your money will also come from somewhere: a job, an inheritance, a source outside or inside of you.

We must learn and have faith that God wants only the best for us. It's in the statement in John 3:16. He sent His best gift, His own Son, to redeem us. "For the LORD God *is* a sun and shield: the LORD will give grace and glory: no good *thing* will he withhold from them that walk uprightly" (Psalm 84:11). "And we know that all things work together for good to those who love God" (Romans 8:28, NKJV). Feed your mind with these thoughts.

It is important to note that though Jesus was God in the flesh, He faced life as we do. He didn't give Himself an "escape from life's problems" plan. He could have performed miracles for Himself to skip His temptations. He didn't.

At one stage, He was *broke*, although all the wealth in the world is His. He needed money for taxes, so He *fished* to pay His debt.

Another time, He was hungry, and the very tree He created didn't produce, so He cursed it. Sound familiar? Many of us curse our situation when we can't wait or can't get what we want when we want it.

Jesus faced everything we are facing and much more.

He fasted for many days; I think it was the longest recorded fast.

They accused Him.

They persecuted Him.

He was thirsty, though He gave water to many who will never thirst again.

He *got angry*, and in the temple, of all places.

The devil tempted him.

He got swapped for a thief.

He was undervalued by one of His followers for thirty pieces of silver!

He prayed for a reprieve from His task. Oh, how familiar that is!

He faced judgment and rejection, and He was spat upon and betrayed.

He was bruised, beaten, and hanged despite committing no fault.

He faced death and the grave and was placed in a borrowed tomb.

After all that, He remained victorious!

He persevered to the end.

Knowing what we now know, we should recognize that the power to persevere is on the inside. Jesus didn't have any outside help; He didn't make any escape plan from His suffering. God walked this earth as a man (Jesus) not only to redeem us, but to show us *it is possible to overcome and succeed.*

I find it's easier to teach someone a task by doing it while they observe. Teaching, you could say, is speaking out or portraying something. Jesus walked the miles to teach us it is possible. He faced His tasks with humility in most cases. He stayed the course and chose. He could have done what Satan told Him to do after His fast; He was hungry. Rather than giving in for a temporary meal, however, He replied to Satan that He was not here for the bread alone. He was here to do His Father's work and to keep His inheritance. Imagine how much He had to subdue His own power to keep the fight fair.

Jesus understands the things we face because He faced them. He walked these same roads, and He persevered. And just in case you missed it, *He got angry.*

You can accomplish what Jesus did. His Word says, "Verily, verily, I say unto you, He that believeth on me, the works that I do shall he do also; and greater *works* than these shall he do" (John 14:12). You can accomplish greatness when you move away from defeating thoughts. Avoid conversations about lack, sicknesses, and problems. If the surrounding discussion is "life is hard" or "I am broke," run as fast as you can away from the spot.

You cannot have success if you are seeing or hearing only failures. Many Scriptures talk about Jesus moving away from the crowd. Some Scriptures say He sent them away or He told the disciples to take Him to the other side. This tells me that sometimes you must move away from the masses, from pessimists. Get away from those who will sink your boat instead of help you to paddle. The conversation in your mind should be of success, not the lack thereof.

I am no expert on DNA and chromosomes, but I know that we have God's DNA in us. He breathes His breath into us. His persevering power got passed on to us so that in all these things, in all these trials, we can be *more than conquerors* (Romans 8:37).

Though not an expert on some things, I am getting to be an expert on persevering. I can wait, though sometimes not patiently.

It is possible to wait for your change. I am not telling you anything I haven't tried myself. I faced many issues, but determination won, and it powers me on to the victorious side.

There are many times when we need that extra motivation to persevere. Sometimes when our goals seem mindboggling. Sometimes when the bills outshine the cash on hand. Sometimes even when we see people who started out after us are doing better than us, or so it seems. When we see others *flourishing*, we may blame our condition and say, "I am failing because of this or that situation," or, "This or that friend caused me to fail." Sometimes we even use the "I didn't finish school" excuse or "I don't have the money to start." People sometimes say, "Lucky you. I am not that fortunate. I win nothing." Hmm. Did you notice how many times in those few words we placed curses on ourselves? If *poor me* is your mindset, don't be surprised if you win nothing or are not fortunate enough to bring about an excellent business idea. After predicting those *unlucky* prophecies over yourself, it's no wonder fortune and any excellent plan have fled. That a business has now set up shop just streets away, with the idea that you thought of, shouldn't discourage you from trying. I have learned that your idea shouldn't be alone. Set up the same business in the area; there is plenty of room for everyone.

Maybe there's something greater for you.

And if you have started but gotten overwhelmed, don't lose hope. Try again. Stay at it a little longer until your desired result comes to fruition.

When we succeed, most of us want it to be known. Some brag, "I did this or that. It was my idea." Yet we don't think our failures have anything to do with us. We don't even realize that failure can teach us. No one blames themselves. You'll rarely hear someone say, "It was my fault." Whether success or failure, you had a hand in the place you are right now.

The Bible says, "Death and life are in the power of the tongue: and they that love it shall eat the fruit thereof" (Proverbs 18:21). And the Bible also warns, "For as he thinketh in his heart, so *is* he" (Proverbs 23:7).

Our lives are the way they are because we are speaking life or death into what we do. The words we utter or think, good or bad, take on life and develop into what we say. "**I can** do all things *through him who strengthens me*" (Philippians 4:13 ESV, emphasis added), is an accurate statement whether you believe it or not. We can persevere through our words, followed by action.

Writer, author, and motivational speaker Napoleon Hill, in one of his many audio recordings, said he had to sit for over twenty years with a list of well-known names that the steel magnate Andrew Carnegie had recommended come forth with the book *Think and Grow Rich.* He had to persevere past his lack of finances, living with his brother, and past some defeating thoughts to believe what he was writing; to change the world and the way men think.

The book did that and is still doing it.

To sit on a project for over twenty years is not something some of us want to consider. In all honesty, some of us will not even do twenty minutes; that seems like a lifetime, given our present financial situation and the hope of finances the project would bring.

Mr. Hill could have cut the project short; according to him, he wasn't being paid. He could have interviewed Henry Ford and ended his investigation; Mr. Ford brought about Ford's cars. Maybe Hill could have stopped at Thomas Edison; the man was successful at failing and successful at succeeding, with over one hundred patents. Hill could have even thought, "Edison failed ten thousand times but kept on trying; now that's perseverance!" That's a splendid story. But Hill didn't stop at Mr. Ford or Mr. Edison. He spent over twenty years writing and interviewing all the influential men mentioned in the book, all the way to an all-time bestseller.

When you think about it, Thomas Edison and many of the world-renowned inventors could have stopped at one or two inventions. However, they persevered.

Here's a thought that should keep you grounded: it's possible to be sitting on the bench of failure even after a tremendous breakthrough, and vice versa. I know I have. I know what it means to persevere after setbacks, disappointments, and failures. If I'm not a good example, then how about the prophet Elijah, who went under a juniper tree wanting to die after he had slain over four hundred prophets of Baal (1 Kings 18:40). He ran to hide because a woman, Jezebel, said she would slay him for killing the prophets (1 Kings 19). You will also find in I Kings 18 that you can try several times for the same thing. Elijah prayed for rain, but it was only on the seventh look that his servant saw something visible. Elijah could've given up or the servant could have stopped looking. A consistent belief that it will work out is all you need.

This book came about because I want to encourage anyone willing to learn, including myself. I have shared some points and seen people's lives changed. Some still haven't changed, but some have. I consider one life changed a success.

This platform will reach a wider audience. Also, making it a book means people will have the *information available on their own time*. This book may say nothing you don't already know, as Ecclesiastes chapter 1 verse 9 says, "What has been is what will be, and what has been done is what will be done, and *there is nothing new under the sun*" (emphasis added), but it is my hope that what is written here will help your mind to connect with your inner self. And as you make that connection, breathe and learn to relax.

You can overcome more things, tolerate more situations, when you struggle less. When you are relaxed, both in mind and body, you have the power to control how you will react. When we worry, we waste energy.

Learn to persevere through whatever is going on around you.

The two blind men mentioned earlier didn't accept their lack of sight as reality.

The woman with the issue of blood didn't accept that she must not, in her state, be seen in public. She had a need: to get rid of the twelve-year-long plague, to rid herself of being an outsider. Who cares about public opinion when you have a need? We do. But we shouldn't.

Press on. Ask permission or for forgiveness; it's your choice.

Pray and press on.

When you have completed those two steps, you can allow *your now* to affect *your future* magnificently. Once you remove bad thoughts, they cease to affect your future forever. It's done unto you according to your belief. You control whether you stop, pause, or press on. If you can picture what you hope to achieve, you can achieve it.

You have nothing to lose if you push on. You have a lot to lose if you don't.

Choose.

> *Every morning in Africa, an antelope wakes up. It knows it must outrun the fastest lion, or it will be killed. Every morning in Africa, a lion wakes up. It knows it must run faster than the slowest antelope, or it will starve. It doesn't matter whether you're the lion or an antelope - when the sun comes up, you'd better be running.*[8]

---

[8] African Proverbs

3

STAY FOCUSED

One of the most important things you can do for yourself is stay focused.

We all have several unfulfilled dreams, but few will pursue them. Some of us may pursue one dream and feel good that we have done that, but what about the option to continue, to go after another? Many choices are before us; we need to think and go after our dreams.

What do you hope to achieve that has seemed unattainable? Nothing is unattainable when you have a definition of purpose and you align it with your dream.

Some of us who have failed at something might think we have exhausted every channel. The one channel that you need to exhaust is to watch the words that proceed from your mouth and what's in your thoughts. When you pray and request that the dreams be awoken, no doubt, you will receive what you have asked for. We think idle talk is just that: idling. But words have the power to create. In the beginning, that was all that was said: "**And God said**, Let there be light: and there was light" (Genesis 1:3, emphasis added).

Again, let me caution you to watch the words that proceed from your mouth. Put a watch to your words. You must speak and stay true to what you say. Stand your ground and have confidence in what you say. If you talk about how good God is, you must not act in the opposite of that statement. If you say, "I will have a magnificent day," act the part. Once you think or utter that statement, stay focused.

Keep your mind from wavering thoughts. "A double-minded person is unstable in *all* his ways" (James 1:8). Stay focused on your desires. Watch for signs that it is bearing fruit, good or bad. Refuse to give up. If you have a thought, a good thought to enhance you and the wider community, make that decision and stand by it. Even if standing alone. Some dreams started on a lonely path. Keep a positive mind centered on it.

A train engineer or operator learns that despite the twists and turns on the track, he must stay focused to get to his destination. He knows it is important to keep the train on the track because lives, not only those of the passengers, but also those at the station, are at stake.

Twists and turns or difficulties do not mean the destination is any different than if you'd traveled a straight path. It just means it may take a little longer to get to your destination.

If you are worried that your ride is too bumpy, distract your mind with the importance of getting to your destination, not *how* you'll get there. In fact, you can distract your mind with how it feels. No one wants to repeat an unpleasant ride, so every effort should be made not to. Your mind will gather strength from what it endures, so give it marvelous things to get through what's going on around you. You may have to think of things you don't normally give attention to, such as thoughts of what you will have for dinner even if it is lunchtime. It is not a wonderful idea to strain the mind with how you will provide for dinner if your finances are an issue. Think past that. Maybe you already have the stuff, so think about how you will prepare the meal.

Think about a jumper in a competition. Whether a high jumper or a long jumper, once he has left the starting line or the ground, he must be committed to completing it. He cannot expect an excellent result if he changes his mind in midair. If he's a high jumper, for him to be successful, before he jumps, he must see himself over the pole. He must see how and where he will land, and that is only achievable by staying focused to develop both his take-off speed and his landing speed. For a good landing, he must develop his inner power, his mind, so that mind, body, and spirit work as one on the ground and in the air. To possess and enhance that skill takes focus.

When your attention is on your goal and you keep your surroundings in the back of your mind, it helps you get your perspective in sync. Once your focus is on your destination, you are well on your way to achieving your goal. Diverting your thoughts to every distraction around you will cause you to miss or lose sight of your goal.

Check your route to see if you are traveling well to your destination.

When a train conductor keys into a computer the route a train must go that day, any deviation to that route warrants an investigation. A deviation to the programed destination could be an unscheduled stop or sitting at a station for far longer than required, or even when something operates outside of its general functions, like an open door or disconnected coach. Those issues set off alarms. The conductor must work every plan and put his knowledge to work to get that train back on the right track. He knows that his job is incomplete if the train and the passengers don't make it to their destination.

You should be so focused on your goal that any deviation from it sets off an alarm in your head. When you're not focused, your mind can be tricked into believing that you are progressing, but that is a terrible lie. When nothing is going on, there is no growth, and you might not even recognize that you are at a standstill.

Keep your momentum towards your goal.

Don't follow wrong paths; stay on track.

True focus will require motivation and reassurance, things that will elevate your mind.

Sometimes, because of obstacles on the track, a train may have to take another route, but that alternative route must still be recorded. Nothing is wrong with taking another route if you will still get to your goal. Learn to cope with derailment and start your journey over. Seek ways to get back on track. Whatever is necessary, do it!

If listening to music keeps you focused, turn it up.

Learn the lyrics to your favorite song so that whenever you can't play it, you can still pull it up in the charts of your mind.

If it's reading the Bible, then meditate on some verses.

There should be no reason you can't find motivation.

Access is available even to the best motivational speakers.

We live in a never-ending cycle of accessibility. There are more social media platforms in this time than ever, and developers are working on other *great* ones right now.

Some years ago, I wanted to go to the Free Chapel church to listen to Pastor Jentezen Franklin. Or even Dr. Tony Evans. Living outside of the United States made it a little pricey, so it was out of reach until an excellent internet plan came along, and then YouTube and Google; now I have twenty-four-seven access to any speaker who has made a video of his or her sermons, with the added channel of Facebook. I still plan to be in the same atmosphere as one of those speakers mentioned, but for now, access via the internet still gives me persevering power.

The answer to staying focus might just be in the minutes, even the seconds, you give an ear to an inspirational message.

The universe is always speaking, even when we are not listening. In the beginning, God created *with His words* (Genesis 1:1). God stayed focus on the plan to create this universe. He is still speaking to us. He never stops using His words. "*In the beginning was the word God spoke*" (1 John 1:1, emphasis added). He is saying, stay focused on My word. I have used My word to form this world, to bring light out of the darkness, to bring land out from the waters. And I can bring you through this. Just stay focused. Your Red Sea or Dead Sea moment is just a process.

When we are focused, we can say to the mountain, "Out of my way, I need to get to my destination." Only a crazy or suicidal person stands in front of a moving train. You are similar to that moving train. When you stand on the words you have uttered, your *mountain* has no other choice but to move. I can't emphasize this enough: stay focused.

The goal of a train or any moving vehicle is to get its *wares* to its destination.

So it is that we must activate the power within us to persevere to our goals.

This world keeps moving, not in a chaotic way where things might bump into things or people into people. You may have gotten a "no" at the bank for your business or mortgage loan; don't let that deter you from getting to your goal. If there are no other banks in your area, move to another area. You are *the client* of the *right* bank.

When rejections appear on your path, don't let them control your mind or your day. You are the one who should control your day; aside from God, only you know what's going on in your mind, and until you say something, others can only guess at what you are thinking.

If you messed up by reacting in a negative manner, don't be too hard on yourself. Learn to forgive yourself and continue on. Spend time daily, five or ten minutes, on staying focused on your goal and your persevering skills; do what might teach you how to respond in another way.

Staying focused might mean staying calm and being still even in the face of danger and disappointment. You may have to stay focused in a small spot. Watch the way the wave or situation around you is flowing and try to relax, and maybe go with the flow. You may also want to have folks around you who will help you paddle on, not ones who might want to tip your boat. When you have the mindset of your surroundings and are aware of where you are at, you'll work better with yourself.

To keep your mind prepared for uncommon situations, test yourself. Give yourself a surviving chance by quizzing yourself. Sometimes you have to stand in front of the mirror and test how you will react if you get a no answer, and from there, work for a yes.

No one likes to fail, yet few of us will give ourselves the chance to win.

Work out the *kinks* that are besetting you.

You may not behave in a hostile manner with your neighbors; however, your kids have yet to see a softer side of you. Try to change that perception. Your mind and body need to travel as one. What we present to a stranger should be the same, or on the same wavelength, as what we give to our family and friends.

Love is love.

It's not the same, but it's not different, either.

Though we may be tolerant of strangers, maybe because the Bible says we might entertain angels unaware, we should still be the same people to our friends and family.

Your action can be the same but different. Start by presenting the same mild-mannered person to those who are closest to you. Make your inner world as acceptable as your outer world. If you don't like how others perceive you, check out the mind and try to renew it. You can change their perception by how you perceive yourself.

Start seeing yourself as the person you would like them to see.

If you find that you are a little *ticked* at your family when asked a question, but you present a different side of yourself to a stranger, either you are bipolar, and I cannot provide a medical answer on that, or you are happy with your delusional bubble. Again, I cannot provide any help or answer on that.

However, if you don't like how you are looking or feeling after an encounter with someone, the best course of action is to work on yourself. Stay focused on what you intend to achieve.

If a better version of you is your goal, you can attain it. Don't alienate yourself from friends and family just because you lose focus.

Stay focused on a better version of you.

> *We must always change, renew, rejuvenate ourselves; otherwise we harden.*[9]

---

[9] Johann Wolfgang von Goethe

4

KEEP MOVING

As not everyone who will read this book is a born-again believer, let me state that we must align our beliefs with some existing thoughts. There is a controller of the universe that led you to this point in the book. I can safely say you are in search of perseverance power; this is why this book found you. And whether Christian or non-Christian, we all need perseverance power in our daily walk.

As the topic says, keep moving; there is no need to slow down based on how your neighbors are doing. You are in control of you. Every action that you do directly contributes to you.

Now, you may think: what an audacious way to involve you in this book! Haven't you been moving all along? Well, let me try to answer this in a general daily scenario, and then you can decide at the end of this chapter and the others if you are *moving with a definition of purpose* and mindful of your journey.

After the things you have done and attempted and the distance you are from where you started, ask yourself, "Am I getting my desired result?" If your answer is yes, without hesitation, you are doing great! Encourage yourself to continue on that path.

If there was hesitation, even the slightest, encourage yourself to strive for a straight yes. Consider what is blocking you, and when you discover the blockage, push through the maze.

While a tentative "yes" is not a major issue, lift yourself to a confident one to get on the road to your purpose. You may just have something great to accomplish, but you must keep moving to make it happen. You can't say you have attained it unless you have completed a journey or a task.

The children of Israel were in bondage, and then they got released. They had to move from Egypt to get to their *promised* land: Canaan. They moved towards the Red Sea, and when they got there, they had to step through it to get to the other side. When going through the sea, if they had stopped, they might have been washed away with Pharaoh's army.

Maybe the only focus of the Israelites was to get out of bondage from Egypt. They cried out for freedom, and they got it, and that was good enough. Seems they didn't want the future that God planned for them. At one point, they wished they weren't free and hadn't left Egypt. As much as they received, they still complained.

In Numbers 21:5, they complained against God to Moses that they had been brought out of Egypt *to die in the wilderness*. That reasoning right there is a defeated mentality. Can you imagine the mindset of these people to think that the God who put dry land in the sea and drowned their oppressors wasn't able to provide *bread and water*! And when He provided, they wanted more. And more. They forgot that before them was a piece of land, *their promised land*, cultivated by giants, with large grapes and milk and honey.

Maybe they forgot that staying focused means to keep going on and through your journey. They seemed focused while walking through the Red Sea. No matter how frightened you may be to do that walk, water on your left and right, an unknown land in front of you and the enemy chasing your behind, getting to the other side should be enough to keep you going.

They may have forgotten that they had to maintain their focus in the wilderness before they could get to the Promised Land. It took them forty years in the wilderness, yet they were still unfocused. This reminds me that throughout school, we hear our teacher say, "Child, stay focused," yet forty years later, we are just getting it.

The Israelites got food, clothes, light, shelter, children, and so much more, all paid for by God, yet they died in the wilderness penniless, so to speak. Not even the Promised Land.

How long can you look at something without it getting into focus or out of focus? If you don't watch where the mind goes, you will lose focus even while looking at a thing. Let me pause here to remind you that your mind will act like a wandering child. Rein in your thoughts. And though something is promised to you, it doesn't mean you mustn't work for it. The Israelites who crossed into the Promised Land, when they got there, had to work for everything they'd gotten for free in the wilderness. No more free food!

What a mindset the Israelites must have been in to be able to look over at the Promised Land but not enter it. It's the same as looking at your business idea or your goal without being able to get to it because you lost focus; the vision or goalpost has shifted, or you don't believe it is possible.

If a runner expects to win, he must keep his eyes on the finish line. He cannot win by looking back at the starting point, nor if his mind is not in the present race or he keeps watching his competitors. There is a famous line: "Keep your eyes on the prize." Despite the tumbles or trips, get up and keep going. A fallen runner sometimes comes back and wins the race. The race is not over until the last runner crosses the finish line.

You may stumble because you're not focused, or it could be an accidental trip from a fellow sojourner. Regardless of what causes the minor *pause*, reset your mind and keep on moving.

I have learned from the Israelites' journey from Egypt to the wilderness that moving is part of growth and victory. Once you stop moving, opportunities will pass you by. The minute the Israelites decided not to go into the land of promise, they gave up their right to be called overcomers or winners. When a runner stops short of a goal, it doesn't matter how close he was to it; the person who crosses the finish line is the winner. The Israelites who made it into the Promised Land *inherited the promise*. For the others, it was just a promise.

If I give you a promissory note but you don't cash it in, it remains blank. You cannot sue the giver for defaulting on the promise, as it was up to you to do something with it. In the journey from Egypt to the wilderness, the ones who stayed focused, Joshua, Caleb, and the younger generation, made it into the Promised Land. Joshua and

Caleb may not have started out from Egypt as decision-makers, but they didn't fall short of making it into Canaan.

It is strange how twelve men went to view the same piece of land but came back with unique perspectives. Ten of the twelve came back with defeated mentalities and won most of the camp over to their side. They said, "We can't go on because there are giants in the land." The multitude accepted their report even before the added statement of "… and *we were in our own sight as grasshoppers*, *and so we were in their sight*" (Numbers 13:33, emphasis added). I don't understand why someone would call himself a grasshopper, but I guess **fear will give you a name if you desire one**.

The sight of the giants may have looked overwhelming, but come on; they could see the land, and it was promised to them! They got so close that they could see the fruitfulness of the land. So, there were a few giants. What of the *multitude of Israel*? They had Jehovah as their Protector, and He controlled the deed to that land. He gave it to them!

But you know, as *funny* as that sounds, I know of landlords afraid of their tenants. So, far be it from me to sneer at the Israelites' minor fearful thoughts. All of us, at one point, see our situations as *giants*. Even the end-of-the-month bills become giants to some of us. We paid them eleven months out of the year, but the twelfth month seems tough.

Anyway, as the Promised Land goes, Joshua and Caleb, the other two of the twelve, had *another view*. They agreed, as the Bible states: "We are more than able to do this [Let's stay focused; let's keep on moving into our promised land]." However, the masses doubted them. The "majority counts" scenario worked against them.

The crowd in the wilderness trusted the message of the ten instead of the two. This tells us it's not always good to have too many people in decision-making roles over your life. Learn to get your own staying power. Decision-making is difficult, but learn to convince yourself *you are well able*. Decide quickly, and if you must, change your mind slowly.

Maybe the elders or older generation who traveled from Egypt forgot that God brought them out; after many years of oppression, through the Red Sea, which destroyed their pursuers. They may have forgotten that He fed them in the wilderness and even showed them the Promised Land. But the mind can be a fickle thing. It sometimes forgets the *wonderful memories* and reminds you of the defeating ones.

Moses, who took on a life-changing job, may have had the awesome task of taking the Israelites out of Egypt, but they had to remain focused. He could bring the message from God to them, but they had to receive it and do as the message said. After Moses experienced what God can do, he seemed okay with pleasing the people over God.

You can imagine that Joshua wasn't old enough to make too many decisions about traveling the route through the Red Sea; he had to go with Moses's decision. However, when his moment came to decide, he said, *"We can do this. We are well able."* He knew that the land was theirs; a promise from Jehovah was all he needed. His bravado may also have come from the fact that he saw how manna and quail fell from above. It powered his thought up to *well able*.

Another odd thing about the Israelites *belief* is that when they were bitten by snakes and God told Moses to make a snake for the people to look at, their stubbornness was unbelievable! They wouldn't even look at the snake.

It goes to show that some people won't even accept help.

After God delivered them, they looked to other gods: metal, wooden, stone...you name it, they *god* it. Everything other than Jehovah God. Their disobedience, disloyalty, and idol-worshipping caused them trouble. Despite it all, God still helped them.

In war, He fought for them. For their healing, all they had to do was **look** at the snake. This action tells me we are very much involved in our breakthroughs (Numbers 21:6–9). Don't just sit still and expect God to do everything for you. He asks, and you do. And sometimes you ask, and He does.

Moving or action is vital to life.

We come alive when we are moving.

If we're fortunate to do so, we wake up, get out of bed, and start our day. Some of us start even before we get out of bed. But despite the disappointments or setbacks of the previous day, we do this; we get moving. Scarcely any thought is given to it; we're on automatic sometimes.

There are some of us, however, who, before we set out, need to have that extra push. This may occur because our minds are stuck in the *gloom and doom* of the closed doors of yesterday.

On another side of the spectrum, some people go to sleep with plans for the next day, so they are moving on waking up. The things they planned may motivate them.

And then there are those "fly by the seat of the *pantsers*": whatever works whenever. The "take no thought for tomorrow" (Matthew 6:34) people. It motivates them to move.

Whether you believe it, we fill our lives with *seeds* of motivations. We all have that *something* that makes us say, "Yeah. I can do this! I will do this! I will get through this." Sometimes we just need something to push us to that point, be it disappointment or failure.

Making it through the day is the most some of us want or can handle.

But anyplace on the spectrum you find yourself, if you are driven in the right direction, that's a magnificent place. However, we can do more than just survive. We can thrive!

We all don't see motivation the same way, but it's all around us. But to get motivated, you must first have a desire for it, a desire that stimulates action.

Take, for instance, when you drive for thirty minutes or more just to get a cup of coffee or tea. What motivates you? Is it the desire for the taste or the picker-upper it gives? Maybe it's the scenery to get to that café. Maybe it is the excellent customer service. But whatever the reason, something pushes you to go that extra mile. That same motivation can work itself into your system. Use the feeling or the drive to push you towards your goal.

Maybe you're not a coffee or tea drinker. What about your motivation to get up and go in search of a job today, though you received several "you're not a fit candidate" responses before? You sent five job applications yesterday, and they were all refused. However, you came across a sixth position, and you submitted your resume. The thought of *just one more time* encouraged you to try, so you did, and voila! They chose you. What motivated you past those five rejections? Maybe it was family to feed or bills.

Think about what pushes you to complete a project; to move earth to get to the finish line. You have a race or a task to finish, and you drive yourself outside of your comfort zone to accomplish it. Sometimes you may not be doing well yourself, yet you try to help someone down on their luck. Could it be a love for humanity? Maybe it is a sense of duty? In any of those cases, we are moved by our motivation. Something had to have motivated you to do it even when your result from yesterday was: "What's the use? Why bother?"

You can move forward, past those thoughts.

Whenever you're moved in the right direction, to help humankind, keep doing it.

Don't forget that motivations can come from both negative and positive issues.

And a positive motivation can send you on a dangerous course.

One example: a child whose parents gave him their all and who is kind to all decides that they were too lenient and doesn't want to walk that route. That child doesn't want to be considered *nice*, so he turns to badness. He's missed the point of the parents' "kind" behavior.

A negative motivation can swing a person either way.

One example is a person who is bullied and who could treat others differently. He knows what it feels like and doesn't want to continue the cycle. In the same situation, another person might bully others because it was done to him. Same situation but different action.

Watch your motives. When you are motivated, watch the direction that motivation is taking you.

If you remember nothing from this book, be sure to remember that motivation comes with energy. The energy is not always from a wonderful source, so it can turn out to be terrible stuff. If your mental part is not pleasant, your motivation can take you on the wrong road.

Some years ago, the acronym M.I.N.D. came to me as Mental Images Needing Direction. Thoughts and images will come, but it is up to you to connect them and send them in the right direction. Your motivation comes from a place that will need you to give it direction. You must find the strength, or better yet, the gumption, to step forward and choose.

Though the ensuing passage is on love, I find it to be a wonderful example of perseverance. Author James Allen, in his *Book of Meditations For Every Day In The Year*, shares:

> You can only learn to love by *constantly meditating upon love as a divine principle, and by adjusting, day by day, all your thought, words and acts on it.* **Watch yourself closely**, and when you think, or say, or do anything which is not born of pure unselfish love, **resolve that you will henceforth guard yourself in that direction**. *By so doing you will every day grow* purer, tenderer, holier, *and soon you will find it easy* to love, and will realise **the Divine within you**. (Emphasis added.)

You can learn to persevere by seeing perseverance as a divine principle and by adjusting, day by day, your energy to act on it.

Persevere to get you to your destination.

Did you know perseverance is tied to motivation? You must be determined or have a determination to go on, to persevere to pass whatever is holding you back. Be ready to do whatever it takes. There is no get-out-of-the-pit-free card. You must hack or hijack your own mind to get it in the right frame to assist you. Your mind can sometimes seem like a separate person. You must get in there and take control.

The word "persevere," as listed in the Online Dictionary, is defined as follows: persevere ərsə'vir/ *verb*: [to] **continue in the course of action even in the face of difficulty** (emphasis added).[10] Some synonyms of "persevere" are: persist, continue, **carry on,** go on, keep on**, keep going**, struggle on, hammer away, **be persistent, be determined, keep at it, press on/ahead, stand fast/firm, hold on** (emphasis added). The Latin *per* means thoroughly, and *Severus*

---

[10] Online Dictionary.com, May 22, 2016

means severe. *You must painstakingly or carefully go on.* Plain and simple.

Despite everything that is going on, in the face of a job loss, repossessed home, and sometimes a loved one passed on, *we must press on.* We must find inspiration, though it may take a lot more than the norm to persevere.

Develop a routine to swim some days in the shallow part of the pool and, some days, to venture out into the deep.

When you find yourself low on motivation, an exceptional place to look is in the book of Job. This book is a *treasure trove*: a secret place of valuable and beautiful things. Job might not have thought that what he was going through was beautiful, but for us, it is beauty-filled. You will find reassurance to persevere. And if you come across those reassurances, keep them; they are yours.

Frankly, when you read what he went through, it should be enough to make you give thanks because your condition might not be half as bad as his. We think that what we are going through is awful and unbearable until…

A quick synopsis of the life of Job. His life came under scrutiny from his friends and family and the devil. He was a rich man; he had everything in abundance. One percent of what he owned was like a thousand percent for most of us. His riches, however, didn't stop him from praising God. He was praising God more to keep himself from presumptuous sins. He made sacrifices unto God daily, even for his children, just in case…

A day came when his entire fortune became *had*. Everything was wiped out; wealth and family! Even his health. Maybe you could say losing his wealth was the worst because it was at the root of most of what he lost. One can scarcely purchase anything without money. Yet even after losing all that, he was motivated to go on, and he continues to praise God.

The Scripture says that each day *filled Job with gratitude,* and he praised God for another day. He never lost sight of thanking God for what he had. His friends and wife pointed out some things that should have gotten him off the *praising path,* but he never looked at his situation negatively. He kept his power to persevere towards his rewards.

However, before I get into the recompenses for his steadfastness, there's something in the story that reminds me that no matter how long a night is, Jehovah will come through. And He doesn't just come empty-handed or without words.

In Job 38–41, you read that if you question God, prepare yourself to get His answers. Next time, chew on this verse a little before you question God: "**Shall a faultfinder contend with the Almighty**?" (40:2, ESV, emphasis added) If you don't like how your situation is, don't find fault; find Jehovah.

Don't argue with God. He is the Creator of everything, including words. David discovered that in the Psalms, as did many kings and prophets in 1 and 2 Kings.

Maybe at your next valley experience, before you ask where God is, you should just "dress for action like a man" (Job 40:7).

I can guarantee you that when Jehovah shows up, it will be in your best interest, but if you have been questioning Him or complaining you might not like it when He does.

Imagine God kept silent from chapter one of the book of Job through to chapter thirty-seven. Thirty-seven chapters of silence! Many of those chapters weren't short ones, either. If you ask someone a question and it takes *thirty-seven minutes* for the person to respond, you will not be interested in the answer anymore. Some of us get bored if we are reading a book and it centers the narration on one person for thirty-seven chapters.

No antagonist or no protagonist? No way would we be interested in continuing to read. Could that be why a memoir is sometimes hard to finish? We want to know how it ends, but if the person's life wasn't as interesting as we want, we give up.

God answered Satan's requests. He answered several requests concerning Job in the same chapter, and even in the same verse, as the request.

Can you imagine: God gave Satan audience! Yet the man that He spoke of, "there is none like him in all the lands," didn't get an answer from Him! Maybe God was showing, to Satan and to us, by not answering Job that there was none like Job. Who else would sit through so many losses other than a man like Job?

Even when Job's three friends and his wife were misrepresenting God, speaking on God's behalf, God kept silent. Just because God is silent, it doesn't mean He's not working things out. Daniel prayed for twenty-one days, and it seemed as if God was silent, but He sent the answer on the first day. However, Satan, that fickle fellow, had a hand in the delay. The Hebrew boys may have thought they had to go through the fire alone. They didn't see God, but He was there.

And here is Satan again, wanting to do Job in.

Job might have come within inches of his life – that's how it looks from the outside – but he was nowhere near death, as God had told Satan, "You cannot touch that part."

There's a Scripture in Job 42 that should be pasted on the outside of all Bibles and bathroom mirrors. It says, *"I know that you [LORD] can do all things*, and that **no purpose of yours can be thwarted"** (v. 2, emphasis added). When we discover such a gem, we should rejoice when facing something seemingly greater than what we believe we can handle.

No purpose of Yours, Lord, can be overturned, hindered, delayed, blocked…

Like Job, if we stay the course, we can reap a reward: great dividends for our setbacks.

The Bible says Job increased in everything without working. Maybe praising God could be considered work. He was wealthy before and after his troubles: *"The Lord restored the fortunes of Job"* (emphasis added). *Restored* means it didn't leave Job; it was just hidden from his eyes, faded a little from his vision.

When an artist or an architect restores a painting or a building, it means they just work on what was there to bring it back to life, to extend life to it for another hundred years, give or take.

That's what God did for Job.

And He gave him twice as much as before! He made what he had shine brighter. Job's faithfulness paid off. His years were even multiplied. *"He lived one hundred and forty more years and saw four generations"* (Job 42:10–17, ESV, emphasis added). Double dividends!

My dear reader, in no way do I want to fool you into believing that Job just got over what he was going through as if someone waved a magic wand. That's far from the truth.

Job, as the story reveals, went through, in human thinking, more than anyone should bear. But despite all that, he remained faithful to his *moving forward plan*.

He proclaimed, "I will wait for my change." It was almost as if Job was saying to himself, "There's nothing else to lose. While I wait, I will talk with the One I know who can change my situation. A change is coming, and even if it is not in this life, I will see Him someday."

What a great dose of inner persevering power!

Believe me; from there, it can only get better. Say it with me, "I will wait."

I wish I could say you can just grab some inspiration and it will be all right. No, that's not even close to the truth. You must want it. You must put some work into it. Remember, when you're going through your *rough or low point*, seek some motivation.

Understand that even accomplished people look for motivation.

Serious dieters look for motivation from a coach, or a meal plan.

An athlete or contestant also looks for motivation in the prize or the accolades that the win will bring.

Think of the scenario where we are waiting for a train to arrive. The train gets to the station, and even though we know it will come to a complete stop, if all the parts are working, we walk to the desired coach we hope to get in. *We move* towards…the desired coach.

Christians and non-Christians seek motivational speakers all the time.

Maybe there's something in us, an innate part of us that craves or desires to be inspired, to be better, to do greater things, to possibly live beyond our present consciousness.

Something gnaws at us to dig deeper, to find some truths to hold on to. No matter how distracted we are at a speaker's engagement or in a church service, as soon as a *special* word or thought is released by the speaker to us, we come alive; we are connected and focused. It may be fleeting, but it's that tiny part of us that was looking for that one word. One thought. Something clicks, which makes us want to shout, "Eureka!"

As children of God, we should keep seeking to keep moving.

Stagnancy kills more dreams than heart attacks do.

The first step to keep moving is to get started. You can't keep moving if you don't start. Giving thanks helps to keep you moving. Be grateful for something. If you are just waking up, whether from a nap or an over-four-hour sleep, say, "I thank you, Lord, that I am breathing." When you are happy or thankful about something, you turn up your boosting energy to give you the recharge your brain needs to keep you moving or to keep at it until you achieve success.

When you have a cold or flu, you seek orange juice; you tell yourself you will get better after a good dose. That's how it is with your mind. It doesn't refuse gratitude juice; it makes you feel better.

Another *hack* to keep going is to get up, get dressed, and move. Even if you are a stay-at-home person, you still need to get up, make your bed, get dressed, go out through your front door and through your gates, and then return home. Moving may just give you some magnificent ideas on how to face your challenges.

The amazing thing about the mind is that it will act independently of you. How is that possible? I am still trying to find that out. But if you leave it unattended, you will reap wild things.

Here's a quick scenario we may all know well. Imagine you are walking up the road and there is no fast food shop on the same street but you want to go find one. You are no longer interested in why you are on that street as your mind sends you off chasing a *scent*. This may happen because your mind is in another direction from your body. If you set out to find something or someone of interest, get your mind on the same track as you.

Stick to your goal. Tune the other senses so they are aligned with your plan.

The apostles, disciples, and prophets listed in the Bible went through what they did, and it is motivation for us. If you read of Elisha in the Old Testament and Paul and Silas in the New Testament, how they pulled through what was hanging over their heads, you can't help but become inspired.

If your goals seem out of reach or you are far from achieving them, learn how to create your life. Pray, sing, meditate, or dance. Do anything you have to do to get encouraged.

Build your mind up with gratitude.

To achieve, we must make our mind want this, too.

It's not how you start; it's how you finish.

At the start of a race, there is a mark showing the starting line. There is also a mark at the end of the race to signal the finish.

For every outstanding thing that you attempt, try to get to the finish line.

If you're faltering, lacking the will to continue, I urge you: do not stay in the *pit*. You're not alone on this journey. In fact, *it is impossible*; God is omnipresent, He is everywhere.

Encourage yourself not to *park* on *despair street*. Don't even slow down; just keep moving. Crawl, hop, skip, or jump if you must. God is with you, before you, and behind you, even when He seems silent. I implore you: whatever you must do, you've got to keep moving.

> *Whenever you have taken up work in hand, you must see it to the finish. That is the ultimate secret of success. Never, never, never give up!*[11]

---

[11] Dada Vaswani

5

HOW LONG?

Let us not be weary...for in due season, we shall reap, if we faint not. (Galatians 6:9)

It may seem ineffectual to tell you to keep moving and stay focused when you must wait, but all three stages will serve you well at the proper time. When you must choose, after several tries, it will come.

For instance, if someone asks you how long you would wait for a change, a promise, or a negative situation to change to positive, what would be your answer? For me, nine out of ten times, I would give a definite answer, something like, "I hope not too long." Not too long seems all some of us can manage. But if you think about it, not too long doesn't have a time limit, either. Therefore, it shows you can wait.

If you have been staying focused to the point of becoming stronger when persevering, you should be on your way, armed with persevering skills, to your goal. When you are at that stage, you shouldn't give up. You are too close. The universe has a portion for you, and you shouldn't settle for anything less.

Sometimes, like the children in the movie *Are We There Yet?* we want to ask that same question. But when a breakthrough comes, you won't have to ask; you will know.

It took some coaching and learning to let go of my timepiece-style of waiting and get on God's own time. There are developmental stages in waiting. His Word says, "They that wait…shall renew their strength." In this stage, you learn to make better plans for what is coming and how to handle it when it comes. Gaining strength helps you get to another stage of your journey.

I like to think I've developed into the person who can wait, and that I can wait longer than I could years ago. There is nothing I can do in the wait except to give thanks, so I might as well do that. The patience part, I am still learning.

Patience, I understand, *is a growing seed.*

Impatience robs you of energy and good growing ability. Nurture patience; plant it in your growing mind. You can lose a lot just by losing patience.

Esau is an excellent example of losing one's blessing because of impatience. Many may say it was his hunger that caused him to lose it; well, that, too, is true. If he'd had patience, he could have waited instead of selling his birthright for a morsel of food.

It feels like no matter if it is one minute, one day, or one month, when a situation is in front of us, even a second seems like a long time. But if you want what you are waiting on, YOU WILL WAIT. **Reconcile your mind to wait with you**. When your mind and body are on two different planets, you will lose. When your mind races ahead of your body, and vice versa, it fills your waiting time with anxiety, and anxiety or anxious thoughts birth no good.

It would be nice to bypass the waiting period in almost every aspect of our lives. Whether it is waiting on a job callback, a date with your significant other, a medical result, or an appointment, *most of us don't wait well.* Our timepieces get the most attention when we are waiting on something or someone.

During our *waiting period*, like Job, sometimes we want to curse the day we were a thought in our parents' minds. Yes, we can be like Job, cursing everything, but never God.

You may notice that this chapter has several questions. I've structured it in this manner because how *you* persevere during the waiting period is important. *The questions are to help you discover your own persevering* or motivating skills.

Remember, you already have it in you. Think of me as being on the sideline, cheering you on with, "You got this! It's already in you to wait for what you want." You waited on this book (smile).

Sometimes you have to wait to get to the finish line.

For instance, if you must travel from one country to another, you will have to wait to board your means of transportation. You may walk around the airport gate or train station and may even sit and read a book, do puzzles, or watch a movie because you would rather wait there than miss your transport. We will even wait, without arguing sometimes, because we have compartmentalized our mind for unfamiliar situations.

When we are paying for the ticket, we may have told ourselves it will be costly to miss the trip. Our minds reason, because of our pockets and checkbooks, that it is best to wait, so we do.

If only we would use that same system when waiting on our problems. Tell your mind it will be too costly to go through that problem again! Distract yourself by occupying your mind with something else. If your present trial is a lack of finances—that's the crucial one for most us—stop feeding your mind with information from broke, going-out-of-business companies. Sometimes their situation is not all bad.

Many companies closed their doors with millions of dollars on their books or in accounts. It may not be the billions they were used to, but it is something. It is not always due to a lack of money that they closed their doors. Sometimes it is because the head of the company has passed away. But leave that information alone and get other inspiration for your present situation. And even if you have a lack of finances, it doesn't mean you can't do something nice for someone. You might just be that person's bread right now. Doing some good will also activate your blessing. "It's in giving that we receive." Don't dwell on the lack. Fill your mind with positive thoughts. One Scripture that is useful in any situation is: "*Whatever is true*, whatever is *noble*, whatever is *right*, whatever is *pure*, whatever is *lovely*, whatever is *admirable — is excellent or praiseworthy — think about such things"* (Philippians 4:8, NIV, emphasis added).

If we are pursuing higher learning, no matter the age, we want to see the tests and the results behind us. We sometimes get flustered, but have you ever noticed that at the end of a test, we may say, "It wasn't as hard as I thought"? All that energy worked up worrying was unnecessary. That's how most of our problems are set up: to keep us distracted. We get so occupied with it that we miss out on the goodness of what's going on. Strive to finish your wait time. Do not cut it short by avoiding it. You may not like the do-over.

"It wasn't as hard as I thought" might be the answer for most of us or for most of our situations. And even though we remember that bit of a revelation, we are still *a worrywart* when we face something new, even when waiting on a test result.

I am not speaking biblically, nor do I have any scientific data or Scripture verse to back this up, but maybe worry was placed in our DNA to help us find the solutions already provided by our Maker. He said we shouldn't worry about anything (Matthew 6). He has already provided (2 Peter 1:3). Yet we read those words, and a few minutes later, some of us will pull out hairs because of a recent issue. Why can't we trust God at His word? We sometimes do, but much, much later.

This is some of us: "I will trust God *after I have tried everything else. Maybe the situation will work itself out."* And then we worry more. Thus, I think the tendency to worry must be in our chromosomes, but, until we master that tendency to stop before we start, worry, for most, is the first course of action. The Bible gives us instruction to cast all our anxiety on God (1 Peter 5:7), but it doesn't seem like we remember that during whatever we are facing.

Life's *swinging door of challenges* does not come with a manual; it's not a quick-read handbook we can flip through. If we are not alert, if we are not careful, and if we concentrate on how things look, it would seem that the easiest thing to do is worry and give up.

It shouldn't be so. God wants us to rely on Him. It doesn't matter if we have drifted from Him; He still loves us and wants to do so much for us.

Sometimes our prayer to God is to *get out of whatever we are facing or move us away from the situation*. But if we can hold out to see how a long a situation will take to change, we see that the hand of God was in it, working on our behalf.

Some of us don't seem to have much of a problem waiting for a friend who is late for the movies or wherever. Sometimes we may be a little *ticked* at a family member, but we will wait on them. We will even wait, sometimes, in the queue at the bank to make a withdrawal or cash a check. Or even in a line to purchase something we like. But we don't want to wait or wait well for God to do what He will *in His time*.

Whatever is besetting us may seem like it's taking too long to run its course, so we get frustrated and go off-course. It's not that we think God can't or won't fix it. Our belief has nothing to do with our perseverance. If that's the case, why do we keep moving even when we don't believe we'll get anywhere? When we are looking at the situation from our standard only, we think there's no fixing it, so why wait? Why bother if the result won't change? It's like not taking our medication anymore because we are not getting better fast enough. We only took six of the twelve tablets prescribed, forgetting that until we take the whole dosage, we will not get rid of what's ailing us.

We must complete the wait time to get the result.

There is no fixed time to wait out, but in case you may think there is, let's look at a few people who, very early in their lives, had big dreams, huge promises, and life-changing visions to carry out, but the answers didn't happen until well into their *ripe* age.

Abraham, the man of faith, will be my first example.

The Bible tells us that Abram, his name at the time of the promise, early in his life, was promised by God to be the father of many nations (Genesis 13:6; 15:1–6; 17:6–8; 18:10). Abram and his wife, Sarai, grew ripe in age, nothing happened; today we would say they were well past childbearing years.

Please note that as much as Abraham was a man of faith, as Hebrews 11 calls him, he, too, didn't want to wait around for what God had promised. If you get a little antsy during your waiting period, don't be ashamed. Remember that Abraham witnessed God working in and through his life many times, yet, this time, he seemed to think this promise was a little outside of God's ability to complete. It seems he forgot who had made him the promise, which also included a son of his own, Isaac, through Sarai.

When his wife didn't get pregnant in the time they thought it should happen, they took the matter into their own hands, and Abram fathered children with other women, with his wife's consent. Would any husband today, unless practicing *that kind of creed,* dare to think his wife would *agree* to that? What was he thinking to suggest or accept such an arrangement?

Anyhow, Abram forgot that God didn't need any help. His one job was to wait for the promise, but though he was a man of faith, he ignored God's promise and took Sarai's suggestion to take her handmaid. Imagine accepting your wife's word over the Lord Almighty. Insanity!

God promised Abram that he would be the father of nations, yet he ran ahead to be the father of a few children and outside of his covenant marriage. Again, in all that, God continued to reaffirm His promise through the years with Abram.

When Abram was one hundred and Sarai was ninety years old, God gave them the promised son, Isaac. It took some years, but they received the promise. God changed Abram's name to Abraham and his wife's name from Sarai to Sarah.

In Hebrews 6:15, the Bible says of Abraham, "After he had *patiently endured, he* got the promise." I am not sure I would use the words *patiently endured* in his case because he went about doing things his way; however, the wonderful thing is that my opinion doesn't count. God is free to call a man what He sees in him. If the Word says, "he patiently endured," there may have been many occurrences that added up to that statement. And might I remind you and myself, as He is God, He's free to name His children by what name He chooses.

Jacob, the trickster, *He called blessed.*

David, the murderer and adulterer, *He called a man after His own heart.*

Abraham, *He called a man of faith and the father of nations.*

Even me, He calls *King's child and blessed*.

It may have taken some years and a few outside-of-the-promise children, but Abraham got what God said He would: he became the father of nations. And God called him His friend. To be a friend of God is well worth any wait.

Another look at a promise being fulfilled way at a ripe age is with the group I like to call *God's band of misfits*: the Israelites. This is a group of *whatever*. They were famous for calling it quits even when victory was at their doorsteps. I can't judge, but it seems like they didn't like to persevere at all! Every day, God had to give them extra motivation. He motivated them with signs and wonders and daily provisions for forty years in the wilderness.

God motivated them by winning battles.

Setting up protection.

Not to mention their seventy years in captivity, when a man called Daniel prayed and waited twenty-one days for an answer for God to remember His promise to free them from captivity.

And even after all that, they still needed motivation, which God sent through Nehemiah.

Isn't that just like some of us?

The plague came, and we didn't get sick, but we still want more.

The locusts came and damaged everything, but we still want more.

The death angel passed through, and the enemy's firstborn died, but still, we want more.

So, we got freedom from slavery, but we need the Red Sea to part. The Red Sea parted, and we walked on dry ground, but we still need more. The enemies chasing us all drowned, but we need more. The manna fell from above, and the snakes were taken away, and we want more.

Then quail and water... So, we came up with other requests: What about leadership, can we get that changed as well? What about freedom of religion, to worship anything, whatever or whomever? We want the fruits and the grapes on the next land, and God said, "*It is your land; get it*," but in this case, we say, "No sa', we are okay here; there are giants there."

Imagine that the land is your inheritance, and all you must do is claim it, but you said no. Maybe you need to see the written deed. Do you want your deliverance or not? Is your belief limited to name only, not possessing? It is your mind, your inheritance, so don't allow *giants* to occupy it. Change your mind, and your actions will change. But it seems it is still not enough.

To this day, we are behaving like Israelites and want the right to this or that! Abortion, same-sex marriages, *sex changes...* Take the chip, don't take the chip.

So, how long?

How about forty years in a wilderness? You may think that is not your reality.

Well, let's say you need a job. You got the job; now what? Now you work for a boss you don't like, collecting less than what you think you are worth, the hours are too long, and...

Let me encourage you to think of your situation in another light. Some people see the glass half-full; some see the glass half-empty. How about a third angle? There is something in the glass, so give thanks.

Whatever situation you find you are in, if you think it is taking too long to change, I want to remind you we have a great "cloud of witnesses" that has gone before us to keep us encouraged. They went through it, and so can we.

Take on the whole armor of God so that you may withstand the waiting days and, having done all, stand firm and wait.

Here's something to remember: when God seems to be late, *we have no real hypothesis of a period of time to accuse Him of; He controls time.* When we asked for something, it was in our yesterday, and He shows up today on time.

It may take some time, but your deliverance will come.

Once more, how long are you willing to wait?

By now, your answer should be: "However long it takes to bring my deliverance."

Starting strong is good. Finishing strong is epic.[12]

---

[12] Henry Wadsworth Longfellow

6

RENEWED EXERTION

Inspiration is everywhere so don't get trapped in reading and watching too much. Get out. Talk to people, friends, family, loved ones. Draw inspiration from everyday life. It has inexhaustible references and is always original.[13]

Inspiration is everywhere! There are so many truths in that quote. One main thought I have gathered is that the author of the quote above is encouraging us to not lock ourselves away when we are in a *low-key* moment, as we do.

Sometimes all we need is an opportunity to move, to get out, to talk with others, to draw inspiration from everyday life. I recommend rest as part of our daily development, and it may sound counterproductive, but to keep motivated, you *must* always rest.

The earth spins nonstop, so we are already on a moving path orchestrated by God. Time doesn't stay still.

No hour, minute, or even second in the day pauses or stops. Each second moves on until it becomes a minute, then an hour, and finally a full twenty-four-hour day. We may pause or stop, but time doesn't. As we keep moving, we will find inspiration to continue.

---

[13] Arnold Arre, comic book writer, "Inspiration Is Everywhere"

Sometimes I have been at low points, even while cheering on or encouraging others to move forward. But I keep doing it because, while encouraging others, I often find something that helps me, that causes me to rise from despair and push on.

Cheering on others also helps me to forget about whatever was ailing me. It may be my depressive or despairing state or my near-empty bank account. *Distracting* yourself by helping others can keep you motivated. It works. Look for something to do or someone to help. It will keep you going.

For me, sometimes it's something on the television. Other times, it may be in a book or a word or phrase from a friend or family. During those *low points*, I keep my ears and eyes tuned to find something motivational that can inspire me to persevere. And I am rarely disappointed. There is no lack of inspiration, only a lack in acknowledging it.

I remember an instance, one Sunday morning, to be precise, while reading my devotion, which was on the life of Job. I have read the story many, many times, so getting this inspiration then was a *sweet treat* and a shock to me. I like to think that if I hadn't been looking for something inspirational, I would have missed it. But I have also learned that you can look at something one hundred times and get a fresh perspective each time.

A new inspiration per se.

Chapters 18 and 19 were assigned to be read that morning, and the words "*power to persevere*" came to mind. I wrote them down. I didn't want to trust my busy schedule or life's distractions; note that I didn't say "forgetfulness." I have discovered that you should always avoid negative words. So, I jotted down the words "power to persevere" because I wanted nothing to take them away. To be certain that those words were fresh inspiration, and that I was being inspired with them, I looked over the chapters and the book I was reading. The devotional is called *Walk Thru the Bible*. I read through several pages to see if those words, "*power to persevere*," were anywhere on the pages.

They weren't.

And so, I rejoiced.

I believe it gave me the power to persevere because of the state I was in; I needed some motivation. I don't know how low my spirit was, but I know it needed a boost. I was going through a series of *misfortune*s, and though I kept it concealed from friends and family, I had hoped that someone could see that I wasn't doing as well as I looked. I wished for someone to offer me something, anything. Who knows, maybe someone did, but sometimes, when you are in a situation of despair or financial woes, you hardly pay attention to what others say.

You must *seek* inspiration, or you might miss it altogether.

On reading further in the chapter, I felt lifted in spirit. Feeling inspired, I started making more notes for a while as the words kept pouring in; however, it was a day to gather in the sanctuary for corporate worship, so I put away the notes and the book and got myself organized for church.

A few hours later, while in church, the moderator of the service raised the song "God Specializes"[14] (see full song on page 117), and wouldn't you know it, but the "power to persevere" popped back in my mind. I wrote the song title down to check it out later to find where it would take me.

As the church service continued, they introduced the day speaker, and the person at the keyboard continued playing. Being a music *connoisseur*, I picked up the tune.

Some people recognize a car by the sound of the engine. Another set of people recognize the sound of an animal or a bird. For me, it's people's voice and music. If I hear a song once, I can pick the tune up again anytime or anywhere. I hope it's a gift I will carry throughout my life: excellent memory and voice recognition.

The tune that was being played was "Whisper His Name," and yes, I couldn't help but jot that down because the *power to persevere* was dancing in my mind. It was as if it was the universe's duty that entire day to make me feel inspired. The words from the devotional and the two songs were connecting in my mind. Sometimes our

---

[14] Lizz Wright, "God Specializes," Metro Lyrics

energy may be low, but if we can just *whisper His name*, we will get some recharging power.

As the day progressed, I couldn't help but think that either my mind was in overdrive or I was on God's agenda to keep inspired, because the speaker of the day took his message from Psalm 46! Was I inspired to write something down? You bet! While the speaker was reading, I grabbed my paper, because verses 1 and 10 of the chapter gave me more inspiration: *helping powers* to persevere.

The verses state: "God is our refuge and strength, an ever-present help in trouble" (v. 1), and therefore, we must "Be still, and know that [He] is God" (v. 10).

It blew me away.

That was what I needed that day.

Be still! *He is God.*

My mind was so fired up that even if I never heard another word that day, that was enough. I was breathing better. I've learned from experience that when you are still, you breathe clearer. When you open your mind to breathe, you will.

Yoga and meditation require that you be still. That is an excellent practice to replicate. When you are still, you can come up with solutions to your issues. In quietness and stillness, we can hear one of God's greatest gifts to us: the air we breathe. When you are quiet, you can even hear your mind.

If only we can recognize that even when the journey seems long or the milestone far away, we still have God. He is ever-present. He's our strength, our refuge, and our help in times of trouble. With that much *firing power* behind us, around us, we ought to persevere.

Inspiration is always flowing, encouraging us to persevere. But if we're *not* feeling the sting of disappointment, the brokenness of hurt, or low in our spirit, the words associated with the inspiration will go unnoticed. It's as if inspiration must come with a tag connected to what we are going through; otherwise, we'll miss it. While our finances are doing well, most times, the average person doesn't look for other ways to get more. And more than likely, we don't need motivation, either. Likewise, when we have a job, unless the pay is terrible or our boss is *horrible*, we don't look for other employment.

If we are not down on our luck, we don't seek inspiration. We don't need to persevere when things are going well; therefore, inspiration kind of passes us by, or we let it pass by.

We get all we need to survive, to endure each day, in that day. If you didn't get it, you didn't look for it. The power to persevere and withstand *whatever* comes with the assurance that your Maker gives you all that you need for the day.

> *The steadfast love of the* LORD *never ceases*; his mercies never come to an end; they are new every morning; great is your faithfulness. (Lamentations 3:22–23, ESV, emphasis added.)

While inspiration is sometimes fleeting, it requires a little more to persevere.

To persevere takes stamina, some motivation, and a powerful will to survive or thrive. It is a strong desire *to stand in the face of difficulties* and say, *though things aren't looking as great as I want them to be at the moment,* my words will not return to me void, but must help me accomplish what I set out to do. My words must bear fruits... *"My word that goes out from my mouth: It will not return to me empty but will accomplish what I desire and achieve the purpose for which I sent it"* (Isaiah 55: 11, NIV, emphasis added).

7

THE EVER-CHANGING MANIFESTATIONS OF FRIENDSHIP

We all have some friends who, by their actions, make us wonder why we are friends, and we all have some friends who, by their actions, make us glad that they are our friends. I appreciate both sets in my life, but I can't say that has always been so.

I have watched my changes over the years with wonder. People I have been friends with for years, and some new ones, I now watch with care how I treat them. Years ago, that was not so. I took for granted that they would always be around, and I didn't have to nurture or treat them as individuals.

They are many friends to me, but I am one to them.

I missed that earlier on.

Each one of my friends, as Job's friends did, viewed my life and our relationship differently.

Speaking of Job, have you read his entire story in the book of Job? I think it is the most insightful book on friendship, loss, perseverance, and self-control. If you're looking for some quick *picker-uppers* during whatever situation, the book of Job is a suitable place.

A line or two from Job's life will help you a long way.

From what they write of this man, it was clear that he suffered major losses: his family, livestock, wealth, friendships…yet he held on. He was certain that even if his flesh failed, he would see his

Redeemer/Creator. He had the confidence that whatever he was going through, his change was coming, so he waited.

Might I add that he waited well? He never complained.

He praised God while he waited.

He pressed on beyond the visits of his friends, who, we would think, came to *encourage* him.

Most of us look forward to the visits of our friends. And like us, Job might have thought, *Great, my friends are coming. It will get better; I feel motivated already!* But guess what? The backup he was hoping to get went in the opposite direction.

First, they came and sat in silence for days, seven days and seven nights, to be exact (2:13). Not even a psalm, hymn, or spiritual song was sung. I'm guessing some people would prefer that their friends use those days to grieve with them or cheer them on. But Job's friends did no such thing.

In time, his friends opened their mouths, and Job, perhaps, wished they had remained silent! They let him have it and launched a magnitude of attacks: ten insults. Along with what he was already going through, he was tormented with their words (Job 19:3), kind of like our own relationships with friends and family. We use our words most times to harm instead of heal. It becomes easier for some of us to say, "You will never amount to anything," instead of, "Wow. You are amazing!" If we realized how much endorphins enter our systems on hearing the latter sentence, we would say it more often. The former sentence draws our energy.

Anyway, let's get back to the book of Job and this amazing manpower. The man was full of problems, but there's something odd, strange, puzzling, even, about his trouble: the God that he thought was his friend gave Satan permission to *bother* him. The funny—not amusing—thing is, Job didn't get a copy of the memo. He was set up by the person he was praising. And the person, God, didn't even give him a behind-the-scenes view.

In the Bible, most people got a warning through a prophecy or even in vision when something was coming at them.

King Nebuchadnezzar, not a man of God, got a script pertaining to his life, even though he did nothing about it (Daniel 4). Even after Daniel explained the script to Nebuchadnezzar, he remained unrepentant.

Saul got a view from his protégé Samuel.

Many kings in the Bible were told about their oncoming downfall if they didn't change their ways. Even in the New Testament, Peter got a memo when Jesus said to him, "Satan desires to sift you…"

However, Job didn't know he'd be the devil's *pet project* or that God had given His seal of approval. Maybe Job would've been a little less *grouchy* knowing God had given His permission. We are more thankful when we know the end results. But despite not knowing, Job held on.

He persevered and remained faithful.

It is important to know that the devil also perseveres. He had a plan to take Job out, so he persevered and went before God, somewhat *barefaced*, as we would say. He came along with the sons of God (Job 1:6). And as they gave their reports, he also gave his. He said he had come from "*going back and forth* in the earth, and from *walking up and down* in it" (v. 7, emphasis added).

It bears repeating that we may want to quit, but the devil doesn't quit. He thought his plan was perfect, so he went before God. It is also significant to note that even the devil had to give a report of how he used his time. He wasn't afraid to give his report and to add it to his plan to destroy a man of praise. Audacious.

He thought he had a wonderful plan, as plans go. But he forgot that God, who is ahead of all of us and knows every step, was the one who started the conversation.

God said something like, "So, you have been busy up and down. What do you think of my servant Job? Have you considered him?"

The question must have blindsided Satan, as he gave an excellent report about Job. His ready answer was in the gist of: "Lord; the man is holy and upright. You are His lofty tower; His shield and buckler, and you are pointing him out. What's going on!"

But he didn't learn; he took the *hook, line, and the whole rod* and asked God for Job's life (1:9-11). Little did he know that he would be the instrument to Job's multiplication of riches.

Job held on even when he didn't know the ending, like some people do. He knew God was in control of the universe. But did he know that God was still watching him in those gloomy days? Maybe not, because he moped.

As mentioned before, Simon Peter, one of Jesus's disciples, knew he was in Satan's radar, as Jesus had said to him, "Simon, Simon, listen! Satan has demanded *permission* to sift [all of] you like grain; *but I have prayed [especially] for you [Peter]*, that your faith [and confidence in Me] may not fail" (Luke 22:31–32, AMP, emphasis added). Did you hear in that sentence, "Don't worry, Peter. I got this"? What's not to love about knowing your trouble is coming but that it will be okay? That's a blessed assurance, an insurance plan.

The interesting thing to note about your situation is it will only bend you, not break you. And we grow stronger from bending and pruning in our lives.

In Job 1:12, when Satan didn't destroy Job in the first deal, he asked for a new deal. This time, God said, "Very well, then, *everything he has is in your power,* but *on the man* himself *do not lay a finger.*" Then Satan went out from the presence of the Lord to carry out his business. He had permission to set up camp in Job's house, and he moved in.

He wiped out the livestock, grains, the servants, and the children.

Job, a man of integrity, did what he'd always done; *whether plenty or empty,* "*Job arose…*fell down upon the ground, *and worshipped.*" And he added to his perseverance when he uttered, "*The LORD gave, and the LORD hath taken away; blessed be the name of the LORD*" (Job 1:20–21, emphasis added).

As if destroying Job's entire stock and children wasn't enough, *Satan went back to God* to renegotiate the contract. The Bible says, "Again…Satan came also among them [the Angels], to present himself before the LORD" (Job 2:1). Then God started bragging more about Job. *He lost everything, but he still called God His savior and blessed His name.*

You know, it's interesting to note here that even Satan follows God's instructions. God told him not to touch Job's flesh, and he didn't. He took everything from Job but left his flesh intact. Another interesting point is that *Satan went back to God to renegotiate that promise,* yet we're afraid to approach God and talk to Him about what concerns us, what we need to be changed in our lives. If we asked for a car but weren't specific and got a *jalopy*, we can go back to Him and renegotiate. It's our birthright to ask our Father.

Satan, renegotiating his promise to God, said: So, I can't touch him, but "Skin for skin, yea, all that a man hath will he give for his life. *But put forth thine hand now, and touch his bone and his flesh, and he will curse thee to thy face.*" (Job 2:4–5, emphasis added.)

I want to pause here for a moment to ask some questions. Why do we, God's children, disobey Him? All that God owns is ours: "*And if children, then heirs; heirs of God, and joint-heirs with Christ*" (Romans 8:17). Why do we distrust Him? Why do we lose faith in Him? In fact, some of us turn our backs on Him.

Disobedience seems to line our path.

Anyway, here's another person who had a copy of the *script*, who knew ahead of time of the *disaster*, like Peter: King Jehoshaphat. He wanted someone to go before God on his and two other kings' behalf. The Bible says that a person went before God and brought back the king a full report, a script he could follow for victory.

How many of us wish to get a blueprint to success?

You don't need me to tell you that you have it.

In the book of Kings, the second chapter, Jehoshaphat asked, "Is there no prophet of the LORD here, through whom we may inquire of the LORD?" He wanted to go on, to persevere. He and the other kings were in a desert, and their water ran out! These three kings, the king of Judah, the king of Israel, and the king of Edom, had traveled for seven days, and someone had forgotten to pack extra water for the journey. So the blame-God game started.

The king of Israel, Joram, exclaimed, "What! Has the LORD called us three kings together only to deliver us into the hands of Moab?" (2 Kings 3:11–10)

If you will note, earlier in the same story, *these three kings agreed* to go through the desert, wilderness in some translations, but now that things had turned a little *dry and hot,* the power of the three, or perseverance, was diminishing.

The first thing the king of Israel thought of was defeat: "*Has the Lord called us three kings together to deliver us into the hands of Moab?*" You have already lost if your first thought is defeat.

May I suggest, when you are at your *dry spell*, don't forget to seek a word from God, and look out for an answer. Even if it is from a passing billboard, a prophet, or an angel, the answer is coming. Look for signs. Be like Jehoshaphat and take the persevering road.

Jehoshaphat's first statement was as if he were saying, *I am seeking a man who knows a God with all the answers; I need such a one to go before this God.* His was a spirit of determination to outlast his *now* situation.

The Bible says that Jehoshaphat sent for the man of God. But as Scripture relates it, it was good to send for the man of God, but it was another matter when that man, Elisha, came. However, before we get to Elisha's response to Jehoshaphat's *friends,* read these verses: "At that time King Joram set out from Samaria and mobilized all Israel. He also sent this message to Jehoshaphat king of Judah: 'The king of Moab has rebelled against me. Will you go with me to fight against Moab?' 'I will go with you,' he replied" (2 Kings 3:6–7).

Did you notice that the battle wasn't even Jehoshaphat's? He was just *helping a friend*!

Sometimes the very company we keep prevents us from persevering. Some of our companies will hamper our ability to move from point A to point C, and the horrible truth is, we are aware of it but hope it will get better.

The Bible says that Joram, the king of Israel, sent a message to Jehoshaphat, king of Judah, saying, *"Will you go with me to fight..?"* (2 Kings 3:7). I want you to pause with me for a moment as I share something else I discovered with that request.

It bowls me over when I read that line, even more so the response of Jehoshaphat. I read it several times. It was an unbelievable request, but the friend's response was even more incredible. Joram did a *friend request*, and Jehoshaphat did a quick *no-hesitation acceptance.* The request and response took my mind to the book of Job. It caused me to evaluate these friendships: the friend of king Joram and the friends of Job.

Unlike the friends of Job, this king, Jehoshaphat, and his friends would *go into battle for him.*

Jehoshaphat's simple response to Joram, his friend, was, "*I will go with you.*" And he signed it with, "Consider *my people as your people, my horses as your horses*" (v. 7, emphasis added).

Job's friends, when they visited him, knew of his situation; he'd even lost things, like family and livestock, in their presence, yet they visited him empty-handed and didn't offer to give him some of their own stuff. But they sure brought a *bellyful of insults.* It bears repeating: sometimes the company you keep prevents your blessings and does not encourage you to persevere.

In 2 Kings, the story shows us that King Joram's friends did the opposite of what Job's friends did. The Bible doesn't mention that the king lost anything; in fact, all the king of Moab did was rebel, yet Joram sent a message to *big brother* Jehoshaphat, who was more than willing to offer his support. He even offered more than requested: animals and people (chapter 3). But as great as the support was from Jehoshaphat, there was another obstacle.

The prophet Elisha.

The Bible states that the kings needed water. They needed a plan B in the middle of points A and C, something to sustain them on their journey. It is impossible to go to war without something as basic as water.

When Elisha came and heard their story, and even though they needed water, upon seeing the kings with his respected friend, King Jehoshaphat, brought a contemptuous look from him. Maybe it was the *defeated speech.* The king said, "[You know what, I think] the LORD, he called us [here]… to deliver us into the hands of the king of Moab" (v. 13ᵇ, emphasis added).

Elisha's response sounds like a man itching to give someone a beat-down. He said, "As surely as the LORD Almighty lives, whom I serve, *if I did not have respect for Jehoshaphat* king of Judah, *I would not pay any attention to you*" (v. 14, emphasis added). The prophet's response was downright *brutal.* But he'd had *enough* and the sounds of those defeated words spoken by a king.

In the king's presence, Elisha said, and I paraphrase: You know what? The only way to rid this place of those defeated words is to praise. "Bring me a harpist" (v. 15). Fill the atmosphere with words of praise.

One can't help but feel revived and ready to get moving, to persevere, after some good, old-fashioned music and a word from the Lord. And be not afraid to get some dirt under your fingernails for your victory.

When the Lord's command comes, whatever He says to, do it. The Bible says that Elisha told them to "*dig ditches!*" And to reinforce them for the battle, he added, "*This is an easy thing in the eyes of the* LORD" (vv 16, 18, emphasis added). That is an award-winning verse for hardship right there: "*an easy thing for the Lord…*"

Be it lack of supply, going into war, or just a purpose to cope, remember, it's "an easy thing in the eyes of the Lord." After Elisha gave them the instruction to dig ditches, those ditches were full to overflowing. Elisha went before the Lord on behalf of the kings and came back with this assurance message:

> I will fill this valley with pools of water. ¹⁷ For this is what the LORD says: You will see neither wind nor rain, yet *this valley will be filled with water*, and you, your cattle and your other animals will drink. ¹⁸ *This is an easy thing in the eyes of the* LORD; *he will also deliver Moab into your hands.* ¹⁹ You will overthrow every fortified city and every major town. You will cut down every good tree, stop up all the springs, and ruin every good field with stones." ²⁰ The next morning, about the time for offering the sacrifice, there it was— water flowing from the direction of Edom! And the land was filled with water. (2 Kings 3:16–20, emphasis added)

It is interesting to note that among the three kings were generations of idol worshippers and other things in the birth line, but God still responded to them because they asked for help. If God helped those kings, how much more will He help His faithful followers?

Maybe that's why, in the face of Satan's brazen request for God to put forth His own hand and touch Job's bone and flesh, he was still alive and was blessed doubly.

When Satan made that request, God said to him: You know what? So you don't think I am a just God? I want you to know, I answer *all* requests. I will remove the clause from the original assignment. You are now free to touch him. "Behold, *he is in thine hand,*" But I will add this new clause: "save his life" (Job 2:6, emphasis added).

Guess what? Satan didn't dawdle, and neither did he ease his assault.

The Bible tells us: "He [Satan] went forth from the presence of the LORD, and smote Job with sore boils from the sole of his foot unto his crown" (Job 2:7).

That was more than an opportune time for Job to give up! He had more than enough opportunities and reasons to *throw in the towel.* He lost everything, even his very skin, and was now repulsive with sores. It seems his support system failed him.

What support system, you may want to know?

The book of Genesis says, "and they become one flesh" (2:24) because *she is* "bone of my bones and flesh of my flesh" (2:23, emphasis added). Job's wife, his helpmeet, who should have been his support system, one flesh with him, who should have borne his sore state and comforted him, said, "Are you *still maintaining your integrity?* Curse God and die!" (2:9, NIV, emphasis added). Job looked at her in a hopeless, helpless state. "Honey, thank you for reminding me about my integrity. I need to keep that." But he wanted to say: You must be *mad*! "You are talking like a foolish woman." Where is your perseverance skill? Where are your morals? "Shall we accept good from God, and not trouble?" Were our marriage vows only for *"better, for richer, for good times, and in health"*? Woman, listen up. I know a change is coming. *"I know that my redeemer lives,* and that in the end he will stand on the earth. And after my skin has been destroyed, yet in my flesh I will see God" (Job 19:25–26, NIV, emphasis added).

After that, it was full speed ahead for this Satan-pestered, seems-like-God-has-deserted widow. Job persevered even in the face of lack and loss.

I don't know if you need any other reminder, but here's another one for the road. This person, like Job, knows what it is to have misfortune but still continue: Jacob.

The Bible says in Genesis 31:3, "Jacob noticed that *Laban's attitude toward him was not what it had been*" (emphasis added). To get to his goal of marrying the love of his life, Jacob had ten wage changes and fourteen years of hard labor. Laban, his father-in-law, "deceived [him], and *changed [his] wages ten times*; but God suffered him not to hurt [him]" (31:7, emphasis added). Maybe the thought of doing Laban harm motivated Jacob to hold on. Vengeance is a potent dose for motivation. Our need for revenge will make us bear suffering to *get back* at someone. But we shouldn't go down that avenue; "Retaliation is mine," says the Lord, "and I will recompense."

It is difficult when the storms of life beset us or when mundane issues seem like a mountain, but I hope this encourages you; if you persevere, the divine plan will work itself out, and for your trouble, it will double the reward! That's a blessed assurance.

Job got it; he was rich before he lost everything, but he got back ten times after. And with two wives, several children, and thousands of livestock, you could say Jacob got it.

All things are there to help us. We will find something to help us hold on even when we don't always see it that way. We might not always get sympathetic support from some of our friends, but there are times when friends like Jehoshaphat come along, who will go with us through rough times. And they are not only willing to go into battle, but they are also willing to share their fortunes.

> *Remember, no matter how fast you run, you can't be the winner if you don't finish.*[15]

---

[15] Israelmore Ayivor

8

BLESSED ASSURANCE

God cares for us. When we accept that the All-Powerful God of the universe is our Father, we will recognize we are well-cared for. Despite the hills or valleys in front of us, we need only to find the power to persevere. He has made and set in place provisions for us no matter where our journey takes us, even if we walk away from Him.

Psalm 139 tells us: God knows when we sit down and rise. There is no place we can go from His presence. The psalmist asked and answered himself: " Where shall I go from your Spirit? Or where shall I flee from your presence? If I ascend to heaven, you are there! If I make my bed in Sheol, you are there!" (vv 6–8, ESV.)

An excellent example of God's sustenance, regardless of where we find ourselves, is the story of the prodigal son, or the parable of the lost son, as some translations call it (Luke 15).

Scripture relates the story of a father and his two sons. I don't know what was going on with one son, or both sons, but the younger son one day said to his father, "Give me my share of the estate" (v. 11), and without reservation, the father divided the property between his sons.

One son collected his share and left, and the other son left his share uncollected.

Maybe some of us are like the adolescent son who took his share and left. God shares His Kingdom with us, but we squander it, and most times, we must come back to Him, and then we repeat the cycle.

I will add that it takes motivation and perseverance to come back after we have wandered away and most likely squandered our fortune. Though you may not like that form of perseverance, on desperate, low-key days, celebrate any way motivation comes. Some days, you must dig in the dumps to get ahead.

The story said that the younger son took all he had and set off for a far county, and there he squandered his wealth in wild living.

When you have a lot of money, you can't help but want to travel far. We don't worry about anything when we have lots of money.

I understand his motive. I want to travel to some faraway country when I get access to money. Money paves a lot of roads, sometimes in the wrong direction.

As this inexperienced man traveled with his wealth, I am sure he felt great. I doubt he needed motivation. Money was his motivation. His motivation was to spend money, to live the big life, which attracted a lot of *wrong* friends.

The lifestyle of the youthful man was great until a famine came. He was in two famines. As the word "famine" means lack, the young man was not only starving for food, but he was starving for motivation.

Many are lacking the *vibes* needed to move forward.

Maybe this adolescent man was in a low state, not just physically but also mentally. To be starving from food is hard, but when your mind is also starving, you are in an awful state.

His state was now that of a pig feeder. And the pigs' food was his meal. In that state, a lot of us would lose our mind, especially if we came from a rich home or a high-paying job, with servants or assistants at our call.

When you're in a *pigpen*, where do you find motivation? You need to do what the young man did: *come to your senses*. Scripture says, "When he came to his senses, he said, 'How many of my father's hired servants have food to spare, and here I am starving to death!'" (v. 17.)

Sometimes things in our past can help us move forward from our present situation if we *do* something. The young man used the information he had gathered while in his father's house to motivate himself. By far, there was no comparison between the pigpen where he was and the mansion where he used to be, but he knew the present place wasn't for him.

May I also add that *though he was in the pigpen, it didn't limit his thoughts*? He said in verse 18, "I will set out and go back to my father and say to him: Father, I have sinned against heaven and against you." What an inspired action it was to come up with motivational thoughts in the *stench* of the location! And his thought process convinced him he would be better off as a servant in his father's house than where he was (v. 19). To get out of his rut and live a better life, he would rather take on a servant's position.

It might not have been how it was when he had money, but it was a better place, and he knew it.

Sometimes all we need to do is just move one level up from where we are. We don't have to get motivation for an enormous leap; just a tiny step will do.

The minute you have a firm will, you will aim to move and continue.

Once we move, we can get there.

Willpower is essential to success.

Not only did the young man create a plan, but he acted on it. He had a set goal: to get out of where he was. Then he acted. He said, "*I will go* to my father," and then he got up and started on his journey. "Only those with the indomitable will that knows neither surrender nor compromise may hope for a large measure of success."[16] The young man acted and worked on being successful before it got to him, and "once the will [was] thoroughly aroused and brought into action, every hindrance in [his] way [was] swept aside."

I can imagine the many thoughts that encouraged him to stay where he was, to turn back, or told him it was not possible to make it back home. Even maybe that his father wouldn't forgive him.

Keep in mind that he was in a far country and had already spent all he had. What little he had collected for tending to the pigs might

---

[16] L.W. Rogers

not have been enough to cover his journey, but he didn't seem to let that hinder him from stepping out. "He got up and went" (v. 20).

When that young man came to his senses and took action to set out on his journey, the God of the universe was already at work, making ways for him to get back home. The power to persevere must be active in any situation. *God works when you move in the right direction.* He can will stuff for us without our participation, but as this is a covenant relationship, when we are ready, God acts on our behalf.

I think the young man saw motivations in the pigs.

By nature, pigs are dirty and disgruntled, and they sometimes act like an unthankful bunch even when they are being fed. Maybe the young man saw how much he had become like the pigs regarding his father's provision. Also, these pigs had someone providing for them, even when they didn't ask for anything. That was the lifestyle the young man had possessed in his father's house. However, now he was dirty, living in a mess.

According to the law of attraction, we create our own reality.

Living in a pigpen might not have been part of his thought-ideas when he was in his father's house, surrounded by wealth and having a good life, but by changing the variable of access to money and bad spending, he thought himself into the *mess* he was in.

But when he acted, after he changed his thoughts, the universe opened channels for him to get ahead and back home. They say, "Whatever you think about and talk about, we bring about."[17] The young man must have thought about his father's house over and over and the things that were there, and as soon as he got there, he got a huge celebration. If only he had known that would be the reception he would get, he would have set out earlier.

Scripture says that when the son was far off, his father saw him and had compassion for him. Compassion means kindness, sympathy, or concern. It is said that half the things we think about never happen. Can you imagine how much the young man might

---

[17] John D Martini

have *injured* himself in his thoughts, thinking about what his father's reaction would be? He even put himself as a servant, which means he was coming to work in his father's house. But when he got there, his rehearsed speech was not even necessary. His father was happy to see him, so he kissed him and gave him the best robe, a ring on his finger, and sandals on his feet. Then he threw him a party with the fatted calf and all the best stuff.

Now that's a glorious end to a rough start. Wouldn't you agree? A pigpen or a mansion?

I am sure the choice would be the mansion any day.

By our thoughts, we keep ourselves from receiving some brilliant stuff! Imagine if that young man had given in to any defeating thoughts that might have come? What if he had stayed where he was? Defeating thoughts don't need an invitation; they will come. Most of us, nine times out of ten, have to convince our minds to move positively. Negativity doesn't need convincing.

Maybe that was what unfolded in the nature of the son who stayed home.

He was still rich. He didn't leave home or take his fortune. Yet even though he had money and full access to the mansion, he didn't feel motivated to forgive or love.

His younger brother had been missing and was now returned, but that didn't mean a thing to him. He was mad that the father was throwing a party with the fatted calf for what he called "a prostitute-using and riotous-living" son.

It makes me wonder if he followed the brother's lifestyle over the years to have known that that was how he was living. Isn't it odd how he talked about his brother's lifestyle during the money-living, but stayed clear of him in the pigpen? Keep in mind that he had his share of the fortune, so don't you think he could have come to his rescue?

I hope you realize from the older brother's action that you must create your own motivation and must not give up. You, and only you, may have to take yourself out of the pigpen.

Don't wait on others to rescue or motivate you.

Don't get bitter and think that's how people are, that nobody wants to help.

They are helping you by not helping. You will be stronger for finding your own energy.

If you don't see an outstretched hand, why not stretch yours out and pull yourself up.

I like what the father said to the *disgruntled* son: "My son, you are always with me, and everything I have is yours. But *we had to celebrate and be glad, because this brother of yours was dead and is alive again; he was lost and is found*" (vv 31–32, emphasis added).

I want to remind you, and myself, that God cares for us. We might feel ashamed or afraid to come to the table and receive what He offers, but we have complete access to Him. This is the God that "can do all things; *no thought or purpose of [His] can be restrained*" (Job 42:2, AMP, emphasis added).

YES! God can.

And we have that power to persevere even in the middle of our nothingness.

Yes!

We can move from the pigpen to the celebration when we change our minds and act.

One of America's largest carmakers, who had a rough start when he started his business, said, "If you think you can or you think you can't, you are probably right."[18]

Can I leave the pigpen?

I don't think I can leave the pigpen.

It doesn't matter the direction you take; the choice is yours. If you think you can't, then stay in the state you are in. *Some people will walk ten miles* to get to their purpose, while *some people won't even drive a mile*.

If you think you can, then do.

Whatever defeating thought you placed in front of your *open door*, you need to know the blessed assurance, the blessed guarantee that your Father is waiting to have a party in your honor and to restore

---

[18] Henry Ford

you to becoming your best self. Persevere from the pigpen through the open door of the mansion.

Nothing builds self-esteem and self-confidence like accomplishment. [19]

---

[19] Thomas Carlyle

9

JUST KEEP ROWING

I am not immune to giving up; I just choose not to. That statement took years to become truth in my life. Hard work and some well-placed *angels* helped me get there and pass some hindrances life tossed on my path.

I have had moments when I've said, "It will get better," to someone and bawling my eyes out in secret about my own issues.

One minute, I was sailing on, and the next minute, I was ready to jump ship. And I can honestly say you never outgrow that rollercoaster feeling; you just continue along the journey and try to make better choices.

I can tell you there is no exact discipline in staying focused, but I have discovered you have to want an excellent outcome and work towards it.

It may be difficult, but keep moving onward no matter how challenging it gets. Find something inspirational, whether a song, a Bible verse, or even a quote you can hold on to during moments of weakened faith.

Don't doubt.

Don't be double-minded.

Try not to sidestep your challenges, either; it will only come back later, and it gets harder. I say it gets harder because anything you skipped or sidestepped, when you face it again, there is a fear in you that you have failed before. This will now cause you to believe, or better yet, doubt yourself that it is possible to overcome. Fear saps energy. No energy, no will to go on.

Face your problems when they come.

Never subtract from your faith. You should only add to or multiply your faith.

To keep going, find some old gospel songs, if that is your thing. We all have something we love to do. Watch TV, listen to the radio, watch the rain… If what you love is good, do it.

There's an old gospel song that I find helpful on my *off* days, during my weakened faith moments: "In this life, my trials are many, and sometimes my feet grow weary, and it seems that I would stumble and almost fall…" The song continues to say that when I stumble, the gentle hands of Jesus are there to keep me steady. He lifts my faith and "gives me grace that I will make it after all." Another encouraging line is: "Keep on trusting and believing are the words I hear Him whisper. . ."

Misery, depression, poverty, and the *kryptonite* that keep us from succeeding, persevering, or accomplishing our dreams have been on my pathway at one point, but I choose to not acknowledge them.

I choose to not acknowledge them means I refuse to talk about poverty or, as much as I can help it, anything in the negative, since I learned that "Anything I think about and talk about I bring about[20]." Also, the Bible says, "As a man thinketh in his heart…" (Proverbs 23:7). Those thoughts keep me from entertaining conversations that cause me distress. Scarcity is distress, and I don't need the misery. I've learned to say, "*I like* joy and happiness," instead of, "*I don't like* sadness." Also, "*I want to have money*," instead of, "*I don't want poverty*." I speak and think of things I like or love instead of things I don't like.

Anything I think about and talk about…

It has not always been so. I have drifted or faltered because of what is going on in my life, things I brought about by my thoughts and actions: stress, worry, or lack of finances.

---

[20] Law of Attraction

Sometimes money *danced* around me instead of settling in my account, so I concentrated on the bills piling up. The thought and the pressure caused me to falter; doubt settled in, rent-free.

It took me some time and a few tests before I realized I needed to stop giving so much energy to the lack. I should instead look at what God is doing. I had to change and train my mind and eyes to see that.

Do you know what is interesting? People saw money on me, saw me prospering, but I couldn't or didn't. It is in such a moment that you can wear happiness or wealth like a cloak. I looked wealthy, even though my bills were unpaid.

I didn't realize I had more access to money or to anything that I wanted. My mindset had to approve the thinking and convey it to the rest of me.

By concentrating on minor things, such as that one or two of the bills were already paid, helped me to know that I would pay the others.

By thinking, *I will pay the bills*, instead of, *when will the bills be paid*? I was rowing to a safe harbor. As a matter of interest, one of my *safe harbor* thoughts came about when I was griping to a friend about paying bills. Little did I know that *going to pay* a bill was a victorious moment.

My friend and I talked about many things, which I've forgotten, but one thing I remember was she asked me where I was going and I said, "I am going to pay some utility bills." I realized that my tone of voice must have been one of *ungratefulness*, because she said, "*KC*, why do you sound like that? Did you hear what you just said? You're going to pay your bills." I didn't get it, so I said, "Yeah, going to pay these bills," and I listed them for emphasis and support. But her support was, "K, you said *you are going to pay*, NOT you have bills and can't afford to pay them!"

I caught on, *repented*, and rejoiced.

I was quite ready for that safe-harbor moment. So now, instead of seeing the bills, I see the money available for them. I'll never walk on that street again, and if I do, I'll get my mindset in the right frame to see the good and keep rowing.

Sometimes my energy or faith is only enough to count the pennies, or in layman's terms, to pinch what little I have to keep going. Though bruised or broke, I try to see that there was enough.

My safe harbor might not be yours, but we all have our "crutches," things we used to prop ourselves up when we feel we can't go on. Mine might be a word or a loan from a friend or playing tic-tac-toe with the funds.

Other crutches could be family, friends, or the job.

Sometimes a safe harbor is used in another form: as an excuse for not following our dream.

There are even times when we don't want to go to church so we use a crutch.

When hindrances come along, I try to find that place where persevering power is already waiting, where all I need to do is show up and pull on whatever source or energy I need.

Years ago, during some of my drifting times, concentrating on anything positive was hard. I couldn't focus on simple things there for my growth. Stable thoughts were fleeting, almost impossible to grasp; it took full determination to stay the course, to get to at least a cruising point. I convinced my mind that church is where a rescue word might be.

My cruising point is that state of mind where I don't have to search for motivation; motivation finds me. It could be something as simple as remembering the Scripture: "Rejoice in the Lord always." That one had a deep revelation for me.

There's a not-so-funny story about that "Rejoice in the Lord" Scripture, which I am led to share.

There was a time when I needed some financial aid. A certain bill was well overdue, and I didn't see any way out. While in my home that morning, I heard the Spirit say to me, "Rejoice in the Lord always, and again I say rejoice."

I said to the Lord, "What is there to rejoice about? I am broke, and this bill is due!" It was about 8 a.m. in the morning.

Nothing happened at noon either, except the Scripture kept coming back in my spirit: "Rejoice in the Lord always…" I stayed at home and cried and moped most of the day as I didn't see any way out.

At around 2:45 p.m., I got ready to go get the children from school, still worried. My eyes swelled from crying, but I got into my car anyway. As I turned the ignition, the radio station that came on was playing a children's program, and wouldn't you know, the children were singing, "Rejoice in the Lord always and again I say rejoice." I knocked the steering wheel and said, "Come on, Jesus!" Then, as there was no escaping the words, I joined in with the kids and sang along: "Rejoice in the Lord always…"

I didn't get to the second line of the song, as my cell phone rang then. Though I wasn't in any great hurry to talk to anyone, I recognized the number and answered it. The person on the line said, "I have a check for you on my desk. It has been ready from earlier this morning. I should have called you earlier but got caught up in meetings." He didn't have to finish the conversation because, to this day, I still think his call that late in the afternoon had nothing to do with his meetings. It had to do with my refusal to *rejoice in the Lord always*, in good and bad times.

I thanked the caller and hung up, got my children from school, and then picked up the check, rejoicing—and I was at the bank, paying the bill, before the end of the day, rejoicing.

As of that day, I've never forgotten to rejoice in the Lord always. Many friends will quote me as saying, "Thankful," whenever I am asked how I am doing.

I have learned since then to always be thankful.

Your safe harbor can also come as a passing billboard. Other times, it will just be a song playing on the radio or even in a commercial on the television.

There are many ways motivation can find you and bring you to that safe harbor, but you have to keep rowing to get there.

Many times, I saw or heard a song or watched a commercial, but at the point I was in my life, something different caught my eyes or ears.

Other times, some situations had me racing to seek the safe harbor, where I would panic to see dry ground so I would row and row and row some more.

Some of those instances where I would seek safe harbor, I would disagree with a friend or family, which sometimes caused me to feel more desolate than an empty bank account. A failed business agreement—no one wants those on their record.

Therefore, we seek. Well, we rush to find instant fixes. We want to control the timetable: when and where it should happen. Most of us have the habit of wanting to keep things in our control, but in most instances, truth be told, we lose control.

Finding a safe place of perseverance won't always happen the way we want it or when we want it, so it is important to make the most of the time and keep rowing.

One way to keep going in such cases is the "lemons to lemonade" *plan*: be grateful for the glimpses you get and then turn them into reminders. They are very helpful on tough days.

If you have been drifting or gliding or in a racing state of mind, at some point, you need to drop anchor. Get your mind to a place where you keep yourself determined that you will not quit just because of some difficult circumstances. Tell yourself you will make it despite your circumstances. Learn to recognize when it is time to anchor.

A boat operator knows it's where and how you put down an anchor, even in the worse conditions, that keeps a boat steady. Note your surroundings and keep in mind where you will let your anchor down. It's very important. Whether it is deep or shallow water, stony or smooth riverbed, test your surroundings.

A boat operator told me that if I plan to let down anchor, I should have plenty of *sturdy ropes*. Also, I should make sure, before going out, that the rope isn't tangled up. It should be clear to perform its duty. You must also look for the smooth bottom of the sea, if it can be seen. It's always good to know whether it's sand, grassy, or stony. A depth-finder can assist with some of these issues.

He also said that if you are in a small boat, you shouldn't just throw your anchor over the side, and a big boat shouldn't just let down its anchor. Your anchor should be let down over the side at the right time. In a small boat, keep your feet from tangling in the rope as the anchor is lowering. He said it is best to stand in the same spot until you have secured the anchor. Wow! That bit of information was powerful. I had to stop and think.

It is best to stand in the same spot until your anchor is secure.

How many of our impatient actions did that thought just blow out of the water, so to speak? To persevere, you must keep moving, but to anchor yourself, you must stop. That sentence can be finalized this way: to make wise decisions, it is best to stop and think.

Somehow, standing in the same spot reminds me of Peter walking on water. Yes, he was doing okay as long as he was walking, but then he stopped, and he sank.

You should learn to recognize what is good for your situation. Is it a "Be still and know that I am God" moment (Psalm 46:10)? Is it a "Lord, 'Bid me to come'" moment (Matthew 14:28)? Or is it a "Help me, Lord, to learn how to wait while I 'March around [my situation] six days'" moment (Joshua 6:3)? Learn to recognize what it requires of you.

Something else I have learned from the boat operator is that you must know the depth you are in to determine how much rope is needed for the anchor. Know the condition of the water and the surrounding weather. Depending on the depth of the water, you measure the amount of rope for the boat to ride the waves. It is necessary to know how much rope to *slack off* [21] so you can drift with the current. Your situation may need a day of fasting or twenty-one days of praying.

When the anchor hits bottom, test the security. Tug on the rope to make sure the anchor is fastened. Once a boat is anchored, you should be able to relax, but keep watching; the anchor can come loose, and you might be drifting.

Not everyone needs to learn how to make an anchor, but information on the process might help you understand how to check your situation. They make most anchors from galvanized aluminum and iron. Depending on your boat size, you need to have the right size or weight. The bigger the ship, the heavier the material needed. What is amazing about the anchor is the rope. The strength of a piece of rope, no matter how small it is, is amazing. Did you know that unless a rope is frayed, if you can't untie it, you must cut it to release it from what it is holding?

---

[21] Moving very slowly, as the tide, wind, or water.

That's the way we should be. We should get our motivation so anchored that nothing can uproot us. You should be at the point where, unless you get your result, you will stay the course.

But it's not only the rope that makes an anchor secure. There's also the chain attached to it. This acts like a go-between between the rope and the iron. The chain has rings attached to the anchor, and there is a slide ring on the anchor bar. The slide ring can slide from front to back, and this is important as it allows the anchor, if caught in a rocky place, to come out.

When you are in a situation, work to get yourself fastened to something that can hold you together. Your anchor should be so fastened that no lack or need disturbs it. When Peter stepped out of the boat, from solid ground to watery surface, he had his faith anchored on "If it is you, Lord, bid me to come," and his anchor was more secured with "Come." He stepped out and started walking on water. He had requested, but he had to get up and go. A movement on his part got him out of the boat.

Have you noticed that if you tell an infant who is just learning to walk to come to you, that infant will get up and take several quick steps? They felt your words, "Come to me," could be trusted, so they moved. But then, maybe the distance between you and them wasn't as close as they thought, so they stopped to think or got a little fearful and fell.

We may need to act out our faith in the same way. Look at your situation and see if it is time to anchor or keep sailing.

If you have to fake it, go right ahead. Talk yourself up until you believe your own words.

Whatever you decide, you must be ready.

Yesterday is gone. Tomorrow has not yet come. We have only today. Let us begin. —Mother Teresa

10

THE TOOLS NECESSARY TO SUCCEED

Now get ready for me to come at you with a series of questions. Be not afraid. They are just there to add a little more wind to your sails.

Are you doing anything about your situation? Have you tried everything possible? How have you been doing what you have been doing? Are you keeping track of your progress? Are you progressing?

If you haven't succeeded, well, I would reason that *you haven't tried all there is to try.* Let me share a story of the persistent widow and the judge in the Bible. We find the story in Luke 18:1-8, in a parable told by Jesus that *men are always to pray and never give up.*

> ² He said: "In a certain town there was not a judge who feared God nor cared what people thought. ³ And there was a widow in that town that kept coming to him with the plea, 'Grant me justice against my adversary.' ⁴ "For some time he refused. But finally he said to himself, 'Even though I don't fear God or care what people think, ⁵ *yet because this widow keeps bothering me, I will see that she gets justice,* so that she won't eventually come and attack me!'" ⁶ And the Lord said, "Listen to what the unjust judge says. ⁷ And *will not God bring about justice for his chosen ones, who cry out to him day and night? Will he keep putting them off? ⁸ I tell you, he will see that they get justice, and quickly.*" (Emphasis added.)

Can you imagine a widow demanding from a king what she wants and how she wants it? Audacious. She was a determined woman.

Author and motivational speaker Napoleon Hill said, "Temporary defeat is not failure until you accept it." My takeaway from that is that it is only when you accept a situation as final that it becomes so. This is not new-age thinking, but if it is, I subscribe to it. You accept defeat when your mind says it is not possible. And if you want Scriptures to back that statement up, there are many. There is Jacob and his wrestling match with the angel (Genesis 28:10–19). There is Joshua and his battle (Joshua 10:12), where he refused to let the sun set and stop him from achieving victory. And there are many other stories, a great cloud of witness.

A more day-to-day example is when you open a file or folder on your desk or on your computer. If you have it open, it remains active. Depending on the result, closing that file could be final or failure.

The widow mentioned earlier refused to accept the judge's answer as final. The story says she wanted justice against her adversary and she kept going back until she got through to the judge. He gave in and said, "Even though I don't fear God or care what people think…" He must have cared what that woman thought and did, because he continued: *"I will see that she gets justice so that she won't eventually come and attack me."* You could say he recognized perseverance.

Children, until they are told otherwise, are excellent examples of perseverance. A child will ask a parent for something several times, and if he doesn't get what he wants from one parent, he will ask the other parent until he does. That child will *pressure* you until you either give in in exasperation or give in to keep him quiet. Children are fearless and relentless. Maybe that is why the Bible gives several "except we be like little children" reminders. They are fearless and persistent.

The will to persevere is in all of us, only most of us are *trained* to be quieter. We're told it's okay to give up if something frustrates us or to turn back if we can't find a way…

You will hear someone say, "It's okay to try again." The part we don't realize is we must continue until we get our desired result.

In the story "Three Feet from Gold," Darby could have given up altogether. He could have even grown resentful that the junkyard man found the gold. He could have also begged for a job when junkyard man discovered it, as he had mining experience. Instead, he took another road to his own gold mine. He created from his mind his own fortune. All the tools that are necessary to succeed are within us; however, sometimes they must come about because of *missed-fortune*.

Many inventions are variations of something.

Take, for instance, the iPhone, which is now famous. Motorola had created a cellphone many years before. BMW also came out with a series of itself.

Maybe the invention your mind came up with cannot come about until somebody else comes out with theirs. Just because your plan didn't work the first time, it doesn't mean it won't work. The tools you need to complete your invention may be with someone else.

Our *microwave lifestyle* tells us that if we can't get it done in three minutes or three tries, then we should give up. That shouldn't be the case. Even the microwave took time to come about.

If we look at some cases in the Bible where numbers were involved, we see that we should not give up on the first or second try; we may even have to go seven times.

There is the story of Naaman, who had leprosy. His helper gave him the solution to go see the prophet Elisha in Israel. The prophet told him to dip in the Jordan River seven times. Being a commander of the army of the king of Aram, at first, Naaman didn't want to do what the prophet said. Maybe he felt it was beneath him to dip into the dirty Jordan River. Naaman preferred the Abana and Pharpar, the rivers of Damascus. He said they were "better than all the waters of Israel." However, his servant told him to do as the prophet said. So, he dipped himself in the Jordan seven times, and his flesh was restored and became clean like that of a young boy (2 Kings 5). From Naaman's condition and remedy, I got an insight: dirty situations are not all bad. Sometimes they can clean us and make us new again.

Another story is of the wall of Jericho. The Israelites had to march around it seven times. The Lord gave that specific order to Joshua. The people followed what Joshua related to them and got the victory. God could have taken the walls down on the first day of the march, even with His own words or winds. Also, the people could have gotten weary when nothing but noise was all they could hear. But no matter how many speculations we come up with, the walls came down on the seventh day, the prescribed amount of days the Lord said.

I am caught up in reading, searching, and discovering ways beyond the norm. I have seen so many doors opened. It used to frighten me to go through them, but now I am not afraid, since I killed doubts.

We have all the tools we need to succeed. "His divine power has granted to us all things that pertain to life and godliness" (2 Peter 1:3, ESV). There is one sure thing the Creator has invested in all humans: a mind. I will dare to say that the only advantage some people have over others is using it.

Look at the many inventions around us. Do you ever wonder where in the mind someone could think of that? I learned that you must see a need to create the thing. Am I looking around for needs? You bet ya.

I have taken to creating some *country-specific books* because the country I now call home didn't have some of those books. Is that an invention? I believe so; an invention is a creation, development, brainchild. And, I will add, an invention is an idea that changes or adds to your area. Maybe that's one reason you must persevere to your invention. Maybe you are thinking it needs to be something tangible or big, like a refrigerator, which keeps things from spoiling, or like a cellphone, which connects the entire world in seconds.

Believe me, anything that you create that is of help to humanity is big.

If you cause one child to think because of something you create, then you have succeeded. That child can create something as well and attribute it to that one thought you shared or caused them to entertain through your writing or art…

If you have gone to seminars, read books, gone to churches, schools, and everywhere the next speaker will show up but it's not happening for you, check your connection.

The power to persevere lies in you. Connect with your mind.

No matter how much someone encourages you, it will be more effective if you accept it as true that you can. Start by changing your mind, which will influence the way you act. Start saying, "I have started the journey," and do at least one thing connected to that *journey*. If you have plans to go on a trip, check out some places of interest. That is action. Not "I will start soon." That way of thinking has no definite plan. It could be today or ten years from today.

If it's starting a business, why don't you check out the costs and the paperwork necessary to get it going? Some might suggest doing a business plan to start. That's good.

Years ago, I thought of a business to get started, and it needed $2,075 to license it, but all I had at the time was $643. After convincing my mind I wanted to do the business, I bought a draft payable to the government to keep me from spending that money. I didn't realize I was activating the power to persevere. A few months later, when the rest of the money came, I paid for my license. It was a proud day to have made such a success. Eleven years later, that business, or I should say that small check of six hundred plus dollars, brought to my doors many other opportunities.

We have all the power to succeed, but if we don't do something, we can't get anything done. If you don't make a move towards your goal, the goalpost will remain within reach but out of your grasp.

An athlete runs towards the finish line; any other action will not accomplish his desired result: to win. In a football match, the object is to get the ball pass your opponents into your net. The more times you do it increases your chance of being the winner. Sometimes you may have to go into the opponents' territory to succeed. God gives us all that we need to succeed every day. But we must accept the gift and try to work on that which we have.

There's a parable told in the Bible of a rich man who was going on a journey. Before he left, he called three of his slaves and gave them different portions of his riches to manage. He gave one five talents, another two talents, and another one talent.

The story says that when the master returned and asked his slaves to give a report, the ones who got the five and two talents had worked on them and increased them. So, the master paid them for their skills. However, the one who had received one talent had played it safe and buried it. According to that slave, "the master wanted to reap where he didn't sow." Then the master said to him that he should have at least invested the money in the bank, which would have given him some interest: "For all those who have, more will be given, and they will have an abundance." The master also called that slave lazy.

Can you imagine? He buried the money to keep it safe, but that was laziness! He also lost his talent to the one who doubled his five talents. The master threw the slave out of the place he was to occupy.

The ones who increased their talents heard the words: "Well done, good and trustworthy slave; you have been trustworthy in a few things, I will put you in charge of many things" (Matthew 25:14–30). Wouldn't you love it if they said those words about you?

It can and will be. All you have to do is to work on the talents.

Even though your day seems dark and the time seems long, remember that the Master is on a temporary journey. He will be back soon to gather His report on what you have done with all He has given you.

Be an excellent steward and persevere to succeed.

11

HOW MANY TRIES?

Tough times never last, but tough people do.[22]

If you are facing tough times, don't miss the lessons that will help you persevere. There are many stories in print and audio about individuals who have given up just minutes or steps away from their goal.

Before we get into some of those stories, remember that for everything you attempt, the decision to either give up or stay the course, you have to make or take on your own. However, sometimes we think, "Why bother?" so we take the easier road and give up.

More than half the time, we miss the *gold* just feet away. The fishermen in the Bible could have missed the catch if they hadn't listened to Jesus when He said to them to cast the net on the other side of the boat. There were many reasons they could have refused. They were tired and hungry, and they had been out all night and had cast the net out several times (John 21:1–6).

Some of us missed the gold because we just didn't try the other side.

One such known story is called "Three Feet from Gold." I label it as a story of perseverance. You can find it in the all-time classic book

---

[22] Robert H. Schuller

Think and Grow Rich, by Napoleon Hill. Many successful people have used and are still using this story as a benchmark to persevere.

The story is about R.U. Darby and his uncle, who had *gold fever*. They set out on their journey, staked their claim, and started digging. It paid off. They found a vein of ore. The story continues that they returned home to raise more money for the machinery needed to bring the ore to the surface. Family and friends invested in the project, so the money came, and they went back to the site to make their fortune.

Things worked out, and soon they were making money to help clear their debts. But then the gold stopped, and the vein disappeared. And after more attempts, they found nothing and quit. They sold the machinery to a junkyard man for a few hundred dollars and left. But the junkyard man didn't just leave the machinery in his yard for another sale; he called an engineer, who checked where Darby and his uncle had been digging and reported that there was more gold in the area—just three feet from where they had stopped digging.

The junkyard man made millions from the mine.

Maybe you could say that it was because he a man who found *treasure* in junk that the junkyard man found the veritable treasure. Maybe you could say he pushed on. Something must have been close to the area where the men had found gold before. Maybe…

Though it was quite a blow for Darby, he learned from his mistake. He became one of the biggest names in insurance and a millionaire in this field. He didn't allow losing the millions from the gold to stop him. He just created another *gold mine*. He learned that you need to persevere through difficulties and stay focused if you want to get to your goal.

Whenever you feel you can't make it, sometimes that's the time to press on more. I have experienced that same feeling a few times, and it's paid off when I persisted. Sometimes I give up, frustrated. But it's even more frustrating when someone else makes it work.

Another well-known story that I find just as encouraging is the story of *Acres of Diamonds* by Russell H. Conwell. The story encourages us to find our acres of diamonds in our own backyard.

The story is about an African farmer who heard tales about other farmers who had made millions by discovering diamond mines.

These tales excited him, so he sold his farm and left. He didn't find any diamonds, so he took his own life. It is a harsh lesson, but sometimes we need that reminder to seek help if a situation gets to be too much. The power to persevere comes from within, but it can connect with someone or something on the outside to pull us through. We can get help if we seek it.

The passage below is Earl Nightingale's take on the *Acres of Diamonds* story. I hope that it will be as helpful for you as it is for me and thousands of others who have read it or are reading it:

> Don't try to run away from your troubles. Overcome them. Prevail right where you are. Triumph over them. And one of the best ways to accomplish that is to get on course and stay there. Restate and reaffirm your goal, the thing you want most to do, the place in life you want most to reach.

> Like a great ship in a storm, just keep your heading and your engines running. The storm will pass, although sometimes it seems that it never will. One bright morning you'll find yourself passing the harbor light. Then you can give a big sigh of relief and rest for a while, and almost before you know it, you'll find your eyes turning seaward again. You'll think of a new harbor you'd like to visit, a new voyage upon which to embark. And once again, you'll set out.

> [We] escape from problems not by running away from them, but by overcoming them. And no sooner [do we] overcome one set of problems, but [we] start looking around for new and more difficult pickles to get into and out of.

> If you feel like running away from it all once in a while, you're perfectly normal. If you stay and get rid of your problems by working your way through them, you're a success. Start taking an hour a day with a legal pad and dissect your work. Take it apart and look at its constituent parts. There's opportunity there. That's your acre of diamonds.

There is opportunity in everything. Some things are risky; some things are for mining. It's up to us to find what lesson is there or what dividends to receive.

About the *Acres of Diamond,* they say that the person who purchased the farm one day found a beautiful rock on the property and he liked it so much that he took it home, cleaned it up, and placed it on his desk. A neighbor came to visit one day and saw the rock; the size shocked him, and also that it was just lying on the desk. He saw the value. He asked if the farmer knew what it was, and the farmer said it was a crystal. The neighbor told the farmer it wasn't a crystal; it was a diamond!

Imagine that! Sometimes we don't know what we have or what is in us until someone helps us. Sometimes a second pair of eyes on our situation is all we need. Though we don't like them sometimes, neighbors are good for us. Maybe that is why the Bible says to love your neighbor; they are like a second pair of eyes.

The first farmer had diamonds on his own property, but he looked for them elsewhere and gave up twice. The second farmer found a diamond but didn't know what it was; someone had to clean it up for him. They say the property became one of the world's largest diamond mines.

I implore you to hold on until you get your breakthrough.

Can you imagine if that second farmer had thrown out the rock? I shudder for both farmers. I wouldn't want to be the first farmer, but I feel for him. I wouldn't want to be the second farmer, either, sitting with the diamond like a pig with a pearl.

The first farmer lived in riches, yet he searched for them elsewhere, gave them up for *greener* pastures.

There is a saying: "Grow or bloom where you are planted." Seek to persevere even when it looks bleak. The *intuition* that there is something there is all you need.

There is another saying: "Intuition is God talking to us." Listen to your intuition.

The second farmer knew there was something about the rock; he just didn't know the exact value. And maybe that's why he held on to it. Until *professional* help came.

The junkyard man sought professional help, and it possibly yielded him a new name: no longer king of junk, but King Midas.

Maybe you are saying, "That's all good and well; those men found diamonds and gold."

Both farmers dug for gold; they did some action.

You could dig in the mind! Your own field of gold. You have countless ideas stored there.

Your mind could be just as fruitful as that of American inventor Thomas Edison, who *filed over one thousand patents for a variety of different inventions.*[i]

According to the information on him, Thomas Edison had only three months of formal schooling, yet his mind yielded him one thousand patents!

Wow.

Some of us could do with just one.

Just one idea, a bestselling book, song, artwork, design…could yield us a diamond.

But there is a part of Mr. Edison's story that you could say made him famous. And in case you think his one thousand patents should have, to some extent, they did. But if you ask someone about Thomas Edison, the first thing they might remember or share about him is that he *failed ten thousand times.* A simple — to us, now that we see it — incandescent lightbulb bested Edison ten thousand times. Come on. A light bulb!

In both instances, he developed persistence, a will to keep going. He knew there was an answer, as he saw it in his mind's eye. He just needed to get the conviction spread to his team.

There are so many lessons to learn from that man's life. My takeaways are, first, after he filed his first patent, he could have stopped and the other nine hundred and ninety-nine would have not come about or maybe would have been accredited to someone else. Second, he could have been satisfied with making his mark with one hundred patents. He wasn't. The third lesson, which is an absolute great motivation for me, is that they fired him from his job at Western Union, after which he developed a product suited for the company that they bought from him, and it made him thousands of dollars.

---

[i] https://www.biographyonline.net/scientists/thomas-edison.html

Losing his job might have caused him to lose a few hundred dollars, but his invention brought him thousands. It is easy to imagine that if he hadn't been fired, he might not have developed that product and his other nine hundred plus products. Even though they said he was deaf, he made all those inventions. He didn't let the diagnosis stop him.

We can persevere despite our circumstances.

The last lesson for this book, about Edison and his ten thousand failed lightbulbs, is that the first time would have been the quitting point for most of us, even the first one hundred times. But failure didn't stop him. He knew the way would find itself somehow. But imagine going at it into the first one thousand times! That kind of persevering power is bar none.

In one of his interviews, Edison said, "None of my inventions came by accident. *I see a worthwhile need to be met, and I make trial after trial until it comes*" (emphasis added).

I have attempted some things in my life, and after about three failures, I would pack it in. Sometimes I picked it up later; sometimes never.

I no longer do that.

I found my persevering power because, one day, I was trying to work at something and I must have tried well over fifty times and maybe fifty different ways, and wouldn't you know it, I got it done.

Another time was after I started writing books. When I wrote *Unlocking the Prayer of Jabez*, I lost the entire file! I took my computer to a tech person, and he couldn't restore the files. I moped for quite some time. I gave up. I told myself, and this may be what a lot of us use, too, "I guess writing [or whatever you failed at] is not for me and that's the universe way of telling me so." How many thoughts like those have you fed your mind?

Anyway, several months later, I started the book again because the book wrestled with me. I convinced myself that if it came from me, it meant the information was somewhere inside of me. So, I persevered. I started writing it, and in less than three days and some hours, I wrote the entire book again! I like to say it is even better than the original.

At least once per day, I try to remind myself, "I will not let this beat me." It became my mantra. The Jabez book was my first published work, and it was well-received. There have been many published ones after that. There are many written ones also waiting to be published. My persevering power propels me to move far away from just one book. I keep going.

There is another story from the Bible that reminds me to persevere and to try more than one, two, or three times. I found the story in 2 Kings 13. It is the story of Elisha and King Jehoash.

Back in those days, it was normal for kings to seek counsel from prophets. Maybe it was respectful to involve the *fathers of the nation* to seek God's plan for a nation. Jehoash was respectful. Jehoash called Elisha "Father." He even cried when Elisha was sick.

The story says that king Jehoash sought Elisha's counsel because of King Aram, who was causing problems. Elisha told Jehoash to pick up some arrows and strike the ground with them. Jehoash did as he was told and struck the ground three times and then quit. Elisha was furious with him and said, "*Why didn't you hit the ground five or six times? Then you would [have beaten] Aram until he was finished. As it is, you'll defeat him three times only*" (2 Kings 13:19, MSG, emphasis added). Note, Elisha said he should have hit the ground *five or six times*. Then he *would have beat Aram until he was finished*. Because he hit it three times, he would only defeat him. I am sure Jehoash would welcome the end of a terrible king any day over just a defeated one. A defeated person can attack again, but if he is finished…that's the end of him!

So, how many attempts should you try before giving up?

There's only one answer. *Never give up* until you get your desired result. You may be just *three feet* from gold, *four days* from resurrection, *five or six* hits from finishing your enemy, *seven dips* from your healing, or, *ten thousand tries* from achieving a brilliant invention. Keep at it!

No one has a problem with the first mile of a journey. Even an infant could do fine for a while. But it isn't the start that matters. It's the finish line. [23]

---

[23] Julien Smith

12

DESTINATION! DESTINATION! REPEAT!

Nothing in the world can take the place of persistence. Talent will not; nothing is more common than unsuccessful men with talent. Genius will not; unrewarded genius is almost a proverb. Education will not; the world is full of educated derelicts. **Persistence and determination alone are omnipotent.**[24] *(emphasis added)*

Next stop…

This was the hardest chapter to write and complete because I had to tread lightly. I had to choose the course to bring us to our destination.

Your destination may be to maintain or increase your goal of persevering. My destination is to make sure this book presents enough assistance to make the journey possible for you to make it to the finish line. I dare not hammer at you; I don't know where the *nail* will land or how solid the wood is. Some people may have been progressing, but for those who waited until this chapter to persevere, it is necessary to introduce more persevering techniques

---

[24] Calvin Coolidge

and examples while presenting some real grits for those who are well on their way. This required a little extra, more than I thought I had.

Writing for both *students* took some perseverance, but it also took what I hope you will gain along the journey: how to accomplish one goal at a time.

If you haven't built up persevering power, I wouldn't want to cheat you of your learning process. Some of us learn a little more *quickly* than others. And if I write that by now, you should be nearing or at your destination, full of persevering power, it would be me demanding that of you instead of you making yourself ready to be there.

My goal is that if this is the only chapter you read, your own persevering power will gain some dynamism. And after the brilliant preceding chapters, I couldn't present anything less.

In fact, anything less would prove me to be less of a persevering *expert* than I *bragged*. I demand more of myself, so writing the chapter four times was a good price to pay when compared to those stories of being *three feet from gold* and suffering *ten thousand failures*. This chapter took a lot of perseverance.

Honestly, I wanted to forgo this chapter. "Who knows," I thought, "maybe this chapter won't be missed? There is enough in the other chapters, if read well, to help one thrive." But then I remembered a quote I read from the author Ernest Hemingway: "Write as well as you can and finish what you started."

Finding that ounce of *genius* required to finish the chapter was so much that I considered it was my test: I can stop if I want to. Do I give up or persevere? Do I capture all the fleeting *not too sure what to say* thoughts and present them as certainties just so I can say I finished the book? I think not! Something burns within me to "finish strong."

Not presenting my best would not be fair to you, and I am sure you would have picked up on the *gibberish*. But it would not be fair to me after telling you "not to sidestep your test; to face it." Also, if I present something less than satisfactory, I would block my future writing and bestselling author's path. I am walking on the path, so I know it is coming!

Besides, I may give you the boost you need for your goals, but you, my dear reader, are boosting me as a writer/author, helping me to keep going. You are precious and important to my growth. We are each other's fans, cheering each other on to get to our destination. And if nothing else, we both can agree that it is important to *finish well*. So, let's get to the finish line together.

I hope the below passage will convey how important it is to complete anything you have started.

> What would you think of an athlete who ran as fast as the wind... for the first half of the race, then walked the rest of the way and came in dead last? What would you think of a baker whose bread and pastries had a marvelous aroma... but upon taking a bite you discovered they were half-baked? Chances are you would look for someone who gave as much attention to the *finish* as to the *start*. In every pursuit of life — whether running, building, baking, or serving God — a job half done is little better than a job that was never begun. (*The Daily Walk Bible*)

A few points to help you thrive on this journey.
Start with a plan for personal growth.

How do I want to accomplish my goal and why? How do I need to accomplish it and why? Where do I lack the will to persevere to accomplish my goal, at the start or is it to continue, and why? How often have I tried to accomplish this personal goal?

When you've asked those questions, put alongside each a number between one to five, one being *not so good*, and start working to get that number higher. You should also remember: your personal growth has nothing to do with how far your friends are ahead of you or how close they are behind you. Your distance and pace are yours to control. If you are moving forward, you are doing something. Your choice to increase your speed is yours.

I sometimes go for walks with friends whose steps are slower than mine and, on some occasions, faster than mine. I appreciate both journeys. It wasn't always so, but when I learned I am being helped in both spheres, I changed my attitude.

I realize that the slower-pace friend helps me to relax a little while I catch my breath and enjoy the scenery and sometimes get a brief catchup conversation along the way. The faster-than-my-pace friend helps me to push past my comfort zone. They get me out of conformity and give me sustaining energy for the next step. The best part is, I am *moving* with both journeys towards my goal of health.

But one thing I hope you noticed is that none of those friends can complete my course for me. I must do it. I can't send either around the track and feel the energy the walk brings. They might describe the journey, but the experience would be lacking. Whatever I experience, I should gain from. Experience teaches. So it is with persevering: you must get through whatever you are facing, your own experience and strength, to be victorious.

You can use money as a superb example of building up your own experience skills because, truth is, we all want more. Even for a millionaire, his/her house costs a lot to maintain. When you are low on finances, if a friend gives you a loan, it is a temporary fix. You have to pay it back eventually, and worse, you might have to pay it back when you are even lower on funds. To be victorious, your next plan or goal is to make sure you become a lender. Set goals to earn more money and have a surplus. It might not happen overnight, unless you have come into an inheritance or win the lottery. But with a personal money-growth plan, it will happen. Do something that will make it happen for you: wash cars, cut lawns, give extra lessons to students about something you are good at…there's a sea of possibility.

Also, another fit place to start is to watch your spending habits. See what expenses you can trim each week from your earnings. And if you find you don't save well, start a mini saving plan with yourself.

One plan that has been working for me is to save one banknote per week. You can teach it to your kids and grandkids, which might break the poverty line in your family, if there is one.

How it works is, decide on a banknote and double or triple the amount each week depending on the week. Week one, you put away one dollar (you can use a five or ten, depending on your goals and your earnings). Week two, you put away two dollars (which makes you three dollars richer by week two). Week three, put away three dollars, and follow the same principle to week fifty-two. At the end of the year, or the end of week fifty-two or your set goal, you should have close to thirteen hundred dollars or thousands of dollars depending on the banknote you used and the timeframe you set. It will take willpower, but it will build perseverance.

You will be tempted to stop the saving plan or use what you have accumulated before it matures, but if you want the fruit of the extra dollars, you have to see it through. "Believe you can and you are halfway there." – Theodore Roosevelt.

Demand it of yourself.

Set a demand on yourself and stick with it. There are countless stories of people who gave up too soon. Don't add to the number. Most of the time, our dreams get parked because we don't place a demand on ourselves, as if it doesn't matter if we succeed or fail. It should matter. And it matters even more to succeed. Many just wish to get through it and hope it will work itself out instead of demanding that it happens. Set the goal, demand of yourself a deadline, and keep it. You can always reset the goal if you didn't make it, within reason, but don't dally or divert far from the set date. If you have moved away from the start mark, push yourself to the finish line. Whatever you are doing, whatever your goal is, stick with it. You can only improve when you persevere.

Measure your growth; it will help to encourage you forward.

Don't be like a person trying to lose weight: exercise and step on the scale a lot and then get disappointed when the numbers remain the same or move higher. One thing that is easy to forget is that your body mass has changed; muscle weighs more than fat.

Remember, developing your *persevering muscles* will strengthen you. You may move slower than when you started; it doesn't mean you aren't moving. It could be you are keeping better timing. "Make sure that all your talent and ability and mentality and ingenuity and vitality and strong feelings – faith, courage – make sure all you've got is being used. Otherwise, you lose."[25]

---

[25] Jim Rohn

The inspiration to give you tenacious, never-quitting power is everywhere. But if we are traveling in the opposite direction than our goals, we will miss them.

Don't wait until you are too far off in the wrong direction. Check on how far you have gone and how long you have been traveling. If you are familiar with your journey, you should at least have an idea if you are persevering or just *malingering*.

When all your energy and persevering power vibrates toward your goal, it will respond with sustainable energy to come closer.

Have a clear direction.

When a person boards a train, it's for one of two reasons: to get to a destination or come from a destination to go to another.

The train you are on may be diverted, but stay focused.

A few meanings for the word "destination" are *final point, last stop, journey's end, and terminus*. The word "journey" means *an expedition, trip, ride, and drive*. So, are you going on a journey, or are you journeying to your destination?

Every day, your goal should be to get to your destination. Remember, the moment you feel you should give up might be the minute or the second you will succeed. All it takes is a second.

Have you ever searched for a particular street and, after a few failed attempts, turned back. Then, when you asked someone where *so or such* a street was and they told you where, when you found it, you realized it was just a street or a few feet from where you turned back? That can be so frustrating. It's a terrible feeling to *almost* find it and then give up.

Almost is never a wonderful decision. Commit fully to get to your destination.

They bound Paul the apostle in chains when he was speaking before King Agrippa and other dignitaries, but he didn't let his situation deter him from achieving his goal. He tried to convince all listening to become Christians. Remember, this is the same Paul (named Saul at the time) who used to even kill anyone wearing clothes that made them look like Christians. This tells me you can be strong-minded. Paul's determination to win men to the call of Christ after he killed men because of the call of Christ was strong.

Anyway, during the midst of his judgment, Paul told the men of his journey to Christianity. They gave him permission to speak, so he spoke of his encounter on the streets of Damascus. In Acts 26:11, Paul says, "Many a time I [journeyed] from one synagogue to another to have them punished, and I tried to force them to blaspheme. **I was obsessed** *with persecuting them that I even hunted them down in foreign cities* [I persevered. Hunting them was my goal]" (emphasis added). Paul had a goal; though it wasn't a wonderful goal, he fulfilled it. And he got good at it, too. But one day, he had an encounter with the Conductor on the Damascus *train,* who gave him a new mission. He shared the new mission with King Agrippa and the other Jews and governors in attendance. He talked about how he had to take the gospel to the same countries and people he had once persecuted. Those people turned around and seized him and delivered him for judgment. Side note: This reminds me that our goals could be as harmful to us as they can be a blessing for us. But whether the outcome is good or bad, we have to face our goals to accomplish them, and throughout the process we must learn.

When Paul finished speaking, King Agrippa asked him, *"Do you think in such a short time you can persuade me to be a Christian?"*

As you are reading this book, I would like to think you are asking me a paraphrased version of that same question. *Do you think in such a short time you have persuaded me to be on the persevering side?* Like Paul, my answer is, "Short time or long—I pray to God that not only you, but all who [will read this book] may become what I am, [a persistent persevering transformer]" (v. 30, NIV, emphasis added). Full persuasion will change your life.

Don't be almost to your goal. Stay the course and finish. Like Paul, you, too, can say, "Whether bound or free, full or empty, I will work to finish. And run with patience the race to attain the prize." (Philippians 4:12, NKJV. Hebrews 12:1-2.)

If you give up before your goal is reached, you are a quitter, and that is the hard truth.

Giving up means you haven't committed yourself to success. A person cannot fail a mission and expect to still get rewarded. Some people board a train with only two stops between them and their destination, while others may have to take two more trains to get to where they are going.

Start at a point: infant stage. Finish at a point: adulthood. Don't remain in the same stage.

In fact, the laws of growth will propel you forward even if you are not reaching your goal or are ready to move; life doesn't stand still. The only sad part is that if you are not assisting yourself as you move along, you might be lost. Or worse, you might get hurt. No sensible person stands still on a moving treadmill. You can either walk or run at your own speed; just set the desired level.

After contemplating all the preceding chapters, I can't repeat this enough: goal setting and sticking to it must become part of your persevering journey. You can only reach your goal if you have a destination in mind. You must know why you are on that journey. Paul was on the road to Damascus because he was going after his passion: persecuting Christians. He was persuaded to attempt the mission, and he went about doing it. He had the power from the rulers and his own goal. That was all he needed. He was ready.

Motivational speaker, Jim Rohn, says:

> If you don't have strong purposes for the future, it's easy to get swallowed by a bad day. It's easy to be almost annihilated by a poor month. And it's easy to almost disappear beneath the waves of a year that goes backwards, if you don't have something to pull you beyond that year.

Your goal should at least give you some persevering power to reach your destination.

You should include persevering in your daily endeavors.

When a person is no longer moving with purpose, one of two things must have happened: he reached his destination, or he has given up his goal and is working someone else's.

If you have reached your goal, maybe now is an excellent time to start another one. That completed goal should supply you with the energy needed to take on something new.

If you are working someone else's goal and are content doing so, who am I to mess with your *idyllic* lifestyle. No one can tell you or decide for you. Only you know where you are at on this journey.

One of the many things I have discovered about a train ride that applies to life and goal-setting is that two people may have boarded a train together, within the same station, but that doesn't mean they are at the same distance from their destination. Some people have miles to go before they get to their destination, while others might just get there on the next stop. If a person has been working on their goal with a definition of purpose, they are much closer than those who don't have a purpose or do anything to keep going. Maybe their perseverance skills have worn thin at the site of a new bill that is twice the size of their income or the one paid last time. Instead of trusting the process, that person doubts and stop progressing. Maybe something we got over last time might be too much to bear this time. This could be based on several circumstances. When you don't get enough rest, whether two hours or six, depending on what your body needs, minor things best you. Keep in mind that whether we are low on persevering power or moving along, it doesn't determine who will get to their goal first.

Aim and achieve.

One day at a time. It is said, "The universe's desire is to give you everything you want,[26]" but many of us don't know what we want and are not sure how to ask.

The Bible says, "ASK. SEEK. BELIEVE. RECEIVE."

There is enough power-packed perseverance power in the Bible.

You need not go back to the old ways of thinking. Stay far from thoughts like, "Well, if it didn't work out, I guess it's the universe's way of saying it wasn't mine." That's a load of manure!

God wants to give you and has given you the keys to the Kingdom. The ability to take failure and turn it into a win IS UP TO YOU.

It's not up to the author of this book.

---

[26] Napoleon Hill

It's not up to your pastor, yoga teacher, or spiritual leader.

It's not up to your parents, family, or friends.

IT IS UP TO YOU!

If you haven't completed your journey, you are assigned a specific purpose, a lot more to accomplish and learn. No matter how much we know or think we know, we can still learn more.

When you are on a train, you don't allow the coach you are in to determine where you are going, so why do you accept that if it didn't work out, it is for the best! Did you attempt to make it work out? How long or how well? Will you allow the stops along the way to hinder you from getting to your goal? I hope not.

Train rides, like life, have a lot of bumps, turns, rattling, changing tracks, all this to get you to your destination. You can complain about the journey or learn to enjoy the ride. The scenery, the countryside and peoples' faces flashing by, can be helpful. The ride is how you view the journey.

The wonderful thing about a train is, if you are on the right one, it is heading in your direction, and if you are a regular rider on that route, you can tell how close you are to your destination. Get familiar with your surroundings. If you feel stuck, tell yourself this isn't your terminus. If, at your last check, you may have missed your stop, get off and catch a connecting one. You must be willing, as you are capable of fulfilling it!

There are lots of lessons to learn from the story of the children of Israel. Every aspect of their journey, from Egypt to the wilderness, shows me ways to *stay focused and keep moving*. When they walked through the parted sea: *faith*. When they slept in the wilderness: *trust*. When they weren't sure where the next meal was coming from: *hope*… And I could go on. But one thing surrounding their lives and action that is still a little puzzling to me is that they left Egypt for a promised land and were willing to go on the journey to get there, but they got worried when they saw it filled with the soon-to-be-previous owners. All along the journey, they persevered onward until they got to see it or got news of the occupants. They risked facing Pharaoh, his army, the Red Sea, and many obstacles, but when the moment to possess their possession came, they gave up.

I still think it was an effortless thing for God to destroy the giants and put the Israelites on the land; He promised it to them. But this tells me that there are some things that God wants us to do for ourselves. He said, "I am giving it to you. All you have to do is come and take it." God moved *hell* (Egypt) and *high water* (Red Sea) to get them to the promised land, and they didn't even walk on it. I beseech you not to get so close to your destination and give up.

The Israelites story gives me a lot of don'ts to live by.

Don't start your goals and then give them over to fear: *They saw giants in the land.*

Don't waste time or energy traveling in the wrong direction: *Forty years in the wilderness.*

Don't feed your mind negativities: *We were like grasshoppers before them.*

Don't follow the massive: *They believed the ten.*

You can well take what's yours. You are more than a conqueror. Walk around your situation or mountain until you have developed the confidence to turn it into a molehill.

When a train is about to move away from the station, you might hear over the PA system the following message: "Stand clear of the closing doors, please." This means you have boarded a vessel bound for one or several destinations, traveling at an impressive speed, so all passengers on board will be safer if the doors are closed. It never occurred to me before, but just looking at the words of the announcement causes me to think of some things that have come to their end in my life that I must let go. For that door to close, I must step away from the sensor. Also, a door closed means I am transported to another stage in my life.

The Israelites walked away from Egypt, but like most of us, who would have done the same, they took the slavery mentality with them. Fear of Pharaoh bound them, and instead of standing clear of the closing door, many of them wanted to go back through to the bondage of Egypt. They would rather trust that system than the unknown.

They say that if you tie your hand to your side for a while, before long, that hand loses its power to operate. The hand, though now loose, has become bound to what it is used to. There is also the story of training an elephant. At a young age, if you tie an elephant to a peg with a piece of rope, they cannot break free. And even when they have grown up (big and strong), the mentality of the piece of rope plagues them, and they never break free.

This train of life you are on is traveling for your pleasure; however, it is up to you to move about the coach and choose your desired seat. Are you going to make conditions or situations stop you from enjoying the ride? I hope you break that thought right now.

When you have developed the art of perseverance, you will learn to relax, read, or sleep during even the most uncomfortable ride. Even Jesus slept on a boat, *during a storm*.

Remember, you can become an undaunted *perseverer* if you allow the power to persevere to be produced. Your goal is to get to your destination; keep your mind in that framework. If you have been through some trials or you have seen a side of failure, still stay focused on your goal.

Not everything attempted will lead to success, but if you have tried it long and hard enough and if success is on the inside, it won't resist forever. You will learn something, whether success or failure. David did against Goliath. Samson did against the Philistines. Job did against his friends and against Satan.

Author, public speaker, and pastor Dr. Tony Evans said, "The worse things get, the closer you are." Don't give up. This may not be true for some things, but it is true of trials and troubles. I find it is also true when you are in the middle of a journey; it leaves you with turning back or continuing when halfway there. You may need to connect with yourself and choose which way to go. When you are between two opinions, you are directionless. Stand still for a moment and, if you need to, ask for help. Ask with authority and determination. The Creator of the universe has placed helpers along the journey.

When you have received the help, keep going until you can't stop. *"Regardless of how dark the night or bewildering the circumstances, it's always safe to trust the Lord."*[27] For a moment, you may have lost sight of

---

[27] Walk Thru the Bible Ministry

where you are or where you are going, but if you have been traveling towards your goal, you should be on the right track; anything else on the track or in your way is just a temporary derailment.

Like the blind men in the story in Matthew 9, you may have to follow Jesus and cry unto Him. Your perseverance may have Him ask, "What will thou have me do for you?" When you recognize that He is the Conductor, your answer should be a confident, "I need _____." You fill in your need. You should always close your request with, "Yes, Lord, I know you can do this very thing." And "Thank you." Always remember, even before the need is met, to give thanks. You may forget to say "thank you" afterward. Showing gratitude is a sustaining energy for persevering power. Fill your life with gratitude.

If you find you get worried along the journey or if you are worried about how you will get from stop A to stop E, keep telling yourself that "the train has left the station, and you are already on the journey. You will get through this."

How long before you are a persevering mastermind? It depends on you. I can say that it may seem like a never-ending journey. But if it seems like it is taking too long, don't let the distance deter you or make it your focus; just continue to persevere. If you cannot get there in the first or second try, just repeat. Perseverance will get you to your goal. Set a purpose to do and do and do again. In times gone by, when we said we were trying, that was acceptable. Today it is best to say, "*I will do* it," instead of, "I will try to do it."

My friend, I hope you realize that you can either dwell where you are and accept failure or you can push into the subliminal mind, the need to continue.

Speaking of the subconscious mind, sometimes you must hide stuff there, away from yourself, or you will be a total wreck. Self gets in our way more often than external entities.

Knowing what we know now, I think you will agree with me that a determined person would rather push to get to the promised land and find giants than sit in the wilderness on a loop.

Whatever you want to persevere to, you can succeed.

Walter Dill Scott says, "Success or failure in business [or any undertaking] is caused more by the **mental attitude** even than by mental capacities." How do you view your ability to succeed? Mental attitude or mental capacities? Do you see yourself at the starting line, trying to build courage, or are you at the finish line, accomplishing the dream?

As you endeavor to persevere, change your perception to see the end of your problem, or journey or whatever you are facing, from the very beginning. While you are standing or kneeling at the starting line, your eyes should already be on the finish line.

In the beginning, God created. And at the end of the six days, everything He created was necessary and good. And it is that same mind He placed in you. Ralph Waldo Emerson says, "A man is what he thinks about all day long." Your perseverance depends on what you impressed on your mind. Will you think of your destination and your right to get there, or will you think of how difficult it will be to get there? Will you persevere past your problem, or will you hold a pity party and invite two special guests, depression and worry?

One last thought I would like to encourage you to take on in this chapter, even if I mentioned it briefly in other chapters: you need to pray every step along your journey. Pray for guidance, endurance, and peace. Pray for your problem and the power to sustain yourself while you go through it. Praying helps in times of trouble, but it will give you peace in the absence of a solution.

May you be encouraged to take your mind to the next stop, the end result of the next gigantic thing. Then repeat. Stick it out. Attempt to reach your goal.

If you aren't getting excellent results, keep at it or try a fresh approach!

If you are still sitting between starting or any excuse, here's the literal *kick in the butt*: **you owe it to the universe to give back!** You were created to create.

Possibility is endless!

Great is the art of beginning, but greater is the art of ending. [28]

---

[28] Henry Wadsworth Longfellow

13

PERSEVERING DURING HARD TIMES

You're going to go through tough times – that's life. But I say, "Nothing happens to you, it happens for you." See the positive in negative events. – Joel Osteen

Indeed, there's no time like now to motivate yourself to persevere, as we are dealing with many *adversaries*: physically, financially, spiritually, emotionally, and mentally, demanding all our *energy*. This is a process, and we should desire to go through it.

When facing any obstacle, *bumpy or not*, it's best to *go through;* going through builds strength.

When I wrote this book, *Power to Persevere*, over three years ago, I had no idea that something as huge as the coronavirus pandemic would surface to the top of things to persevere through. Sure, I was encouraging us to persevere regardless of our situation, financial or physical, or during a little doubtful moment, but the turn of the pandemic, I would say, moved us from the kiddies' pool straight into the ocean, like young birds thrown from the mother's nest.

I think it's safe to say that none of us expected this. And it's also safe to say that before the pandemic, some of us were in planning-summer-vacation mode. Some were preparing for Easter break.

Churches were planning to celebrate the death and resurrection of our Savior, and students were getting ready for graduations, final exams, and, and…

We all had many plans, but all or most of them seemed to have been for zilch.

I can't help but add a little *Caribbean* humor I heard a lot growing up. It goes, "Man plan; God wipe out." It means that many of our plans don't come to fruition because God knows best what is good for us. His plans for us are for life. Jeremiah 29:11 states, "For **I know the plans I have for you**, declares the LORD, **plans for welfare** and not for evil, **to give you a future and a hope**" (ESV, emphasis added). He adjusts our sails when we stray off-track.

We make many plans, but very few are in our *best* interest.

Relating to this book, it was my plan to publish it in early 2020, but I don't need to tell you that things changed, personally, emotionally, and financially. I am sure those changes are not unique to me as the coronavirus swept through, or better stated, took up habitation on our planet. No country, it seems, was exempted; everyone everywhere was affected.

Many have lost families, friends, jobs, and their comforts; they can't do what they want to when they want. Some people got sick and recovered and then sick again. Some people find it hard to live with something that seems to have no cure in sight. The worst part is, the coronavirus mimics the common cold—sneezing, coughing, headaches—which should make curing it a *breeze*. But not so. However, it is our hope not to be beaten by it.

It seems no matter how many years you have been working or going to school, with this pandemic, you've had to learn new ways of doing these things, even new ways to spend time with family, and in some cases, without family, as some were stuck in faraway countries or got sick and quarantined and many other things. Even cash-flow and shopping have become educational; well, for me. I had to learn to use less money to get more supplies.

On a regular day, we may not like changes, but we've had to adapt in this crisis.

School time was interrupted, so students had to start a new way of learning. Maybe before the pandemic, many parents or guardians were encouraging children to spend less time on computers, cellphones, and tablets. Not so anymore.

But in all this *new normalcy,* maybe the hardest thing to cope with is **fear**.

It is no secret; more people die from fear than what is facing them. We all fear the unknown.

Questions and doubts may fill our minds: When will this end? Will it end? What about my job? My finances? Will my business recover? My family? My friends? And the list goes on.

We may think we are not anxious, but if we were to examine our reaction or behavior, we might see hints or traces of fear and doubt.

To be honest, in the beginning of the pandemic, I had some doubts; my faith got shaken. Believe me, doubts, even in small doses, can destroy the mightiest warrior; we shouldn't encourage it to tarry in our domain.

Never would I have imagined a day, especially in a free country, when the doors of churches would be closed; every day. In all my growing-up years, and I did a lot of growing up, I never saw the doors of churches closed unless it was not a day of worship. So, with that new issue thrown into the midst of the pandemic, fear came. But thankfully, my fears were calmed when I discovered that even though we couldn't physically go into the sanctuary, a deeper chapter has begun with churches online. I've enjoyed it, especially learning more of the Word of God.

Another fear-driver in this pandemic is social distancing. *Social* should not be used along with the word *distancing*. This is just my opinion. We may not speak all the time to our neighbors, but community involvement is how most of us strive. We laugh and share backyard barbeques and games. Rekindling community vibes should be on our post-pandemic list.

Maybe some of our fears come about because we no longer have the freedom to travel at will, something some of us love to do but may have taken for granted.

Our fears may have grown because we've lost family and friends. We fear money going out and, in some cases, nothing coming in. Maybe fear also stems from the fact that we may have thought this was a temporary thing but, months later, we are no closer to the end. We may fear because our actions, or lack thereof, could bring home the virus. We also fear border closures, no flights. And there are many other fear-stemming issues.

I want to remind you, if you feed your fear, it will grow like a wild weed.

If not reined in, it could overtake your mind and entire life.

But there is hope.

Help is available.

We can persevere during any pandemic, epidemic, or mountain-trembling issue if we can remember that "fear is removable."[29] You can silence your fear. God has not given us a spirit of fear or timidity… but of love and of a **sound mind** (2 Timothy 1:7). Some Bible translations use "self-discipline." We need self-discipline in this and any difficult time. Though we are tested, we should persevere to control our feelings in any crisis to overcome.

Make every effort not to let fear in. However, if it gets in, remember, it is removable.

King Solomon, in Ecclesiastes 3, says, "There's a time for everything." Nothing is set. I constantly remind myself that the earth rotates, and nothing can stop it from doing it. So, when a situation is in front of me, very soon, it will be behind me. It only stays in front of me if I keep turning to look at it or I keep my mind on it.

Author and motivational speaker Norman Vincent Peale said, "A primary fact that we need to know about anxiety and fear is that they are removable. Any emotion is removable. Anger is removable. Depression is removable… The first step in overcoming any fear is to realize that it is, for a fact, removable." He goes on to say that "once you know that fear is removable, next comes the process of removing it."

---

[29] Norman Vincent Peale

Everything in this world exists by order. Even in what seems like a chaotic moment, God is still in control. Everything is subjected to His divine will and purpose. In Job 38, the Bible says, "God tells everything where they must go." It doesn't matter if you are going through a pandemic, a financial setback, or just a fearful moment; you have what it takes to survive.

For you to eliminate fear from your life, to persevere to a better normalcy in your *atmosphere* where you control your reaction, you have to exercise self-discipline or willpower.

In this pandemic, because of rules, you have to discipline yourself to stay at home, even when you are itching to go *knock-about*. Many countries have included curfew times and day trips by surnames to their recovery plan, and though you may want to be the *boss* of your day, you try to abide by them, a learned discipline. You are managing.

Therefore, don't be hard on yourself if fear comes.

As a matter of fact, as long as you are alive, you will have reasons to fear. But on the flip side of that, as long as you are alive, you will have reasons to hope.

Also, you are not alone in your fear. Some of the greatest warriors, leaders, and pastors will admit that at one point, a bit of fear settled in their system. It's natural to fear. But you can stop yourself from getting overwhelmed.

When you give in to fear, you are allowing it to infiltrate or take root. When something takes root, it gets more difficult to remove. It will take more than *mere* persevering to get back in your right mind. If fear settles in, you will have to give it your all, to clear it from your pathway. A strong will or willpower needs time to build up, so work on what got you to this point to get to the next.

What will help you, is to tell yourself you have survived or pulled through other things and will continue to survive as long as you do not give up. This pandemic may not measure up to World War II or the Holocaust experience, but people have survived them, so you can survive this.

Your situation is not unique. Fear is not new.

Fear will attack the timidest and the bravest amongst us; it just needs an inroad. Former US president Theodore Roosevelt said, "I have often been afraid, but I wouldn't give in to it. I made myself act as though I was not afraid, and gradually my fear disappeared." Think courageous thoughts and act accordingly, and you will control and finally remove your fear.

It will not be easy, but if it wasn't possible, the Creator wouldn't have allowed fear in the universe. He completes everything that He started. "God gives the trouble and the cure."[30]

Eleanor Roosevelt said, "You gain strength, courage, and confidence by every experience in which you look fear in the face." Be brave. Take a step forward and start owning the fact there is an ounce of *super* power in you: the power to persevere. Mrs. Roosevelt also said, "No one can make you feel inferior without your consent." Not even fear can make you feel inferior without your consent.

I will say again for emphasis, do not fuel your fear. Don't let fear take root in your mind. You have a job to do now. Don't worry about a future job. Accept the job that is given to you: the job to stay strong and courageous now. Someone somewhere is waiting on your success to get them through what they are facing. Whether COVID-19, financial struggle, unemployment, whatever your fear is, you can and will get through it.

The power to persevere is yours to control.

The Bible says, "Men's hearts failing them for fear, *and for looking after those things which are coming on the earth…*" (Luke 21:26, emphasis added). This new pandemic is certainly something that came on this earth and is causing fear; however, the Bible also gives us a remedy that we should "always pray, and not to give up" (Luke 18:1). Take heart; know that you can develop strength even in the face of fear. You can stop and banish what is causing you to fear. *Don't dwell* on your current situation and *believe in* the outcome; you will get through this.

I read an article on some thoughts to think about when facing fear. It said, "Every human being has to decide again and again whether to meet fearsome difficulties head-on or to try running away."[31] The

---

[30] The movie *Resurrection*, 2018
[31] "Jack's Insights: Life Lessons Learned from Hereford Cows"

thought that "we have to decide again and again" jolted my senses. It's a good feeling to know the decision is up to you whether to fear. The article went on to say:

> You can never outrun fear. Try it and you will run yourself down, a pathetic victim of anxiety. Try a better way. Take a long, searching look at your fear. Stand up to it. It probably won't happen anyway. And if it does, you have what it takes to meet it and successfully control it.

I think that is a really honest approach to fear. It is best to deal with fear head on. Recognize what is causing the fear and deal with it. Another thought from another article states, "We all go through tough times; it's inevitable," but we can use these tips to get us through some of those times:

1. Stick to a routine. Maintaining your to-do list during difficult times will give you purpose and help you make progress.
2. Practice self-care. Being kind to yourself is one of the most important things to do when you're down.
3. Reach out to loved ones. The support of friends and family will keep you from feeling alone when life is tough.[ii]

I will admit it is hard to tell you how to feel or how you are supposed to feel during your situation. Your experience is your own. How well you cope is all up to you, but we all can accept a little coaching; everyone can do with some inspiration.

If fear is causing you to feel overwhelmed, take a respite; we can get solutions to our problems when we pause for a moment. A fresh look at something reveals new ideas or solutions. Many times, you may feel exhausted as the situation seems hopeless, but I dare you to look away for a minute. When you look back at the situation, expect the best outcome. Consider there is a lesson to be learned from your

---

[ii] www.thoughtsabove.com

situation and learn it. You have the resourcefulness to be in this fight; tough it up. It is not a time to give up or show weakness.

I am not saying you shouldn't cry.

In fact, I think you should have a big *bawl*. Give yourself the moment to be human. Your situation, whatever it is, may be hard for you for a little while until you clear yourself from the fear that is holding you back from succeeding. In crying, you remove the built-up stress and feeling of hopelessness. A few teary moments are recommended on any given day. You have the opportunity to *feel*, to connect to your emotion. However, watch out for the pitfalls of staying in a teary moment too long. It is easy to cry yourself to freedom, but it's even easier to cry yourself to depression. You choose. A good measuring cup in life is to use moderation. Cry, but to a point.

Make every effort to feed your mind positive things. There is an oasis of affirmations, inspirational songs and Bible verses available around you.

What am I saying? What can you possibly gain from this book?

I hope I will at least help you to learn two things.

First, in any condition that seems to want to sap your energy or the very hope you are holding on to, choose to persevere. *Your decision* to stand strong is a way to outlast your problem. Face your fear. Acknowledge that you are afraid so that you can conquer that fear.

Second, your situation is not problematic; you are. It is the truth that we most try to avoid, but it is true. You are the person who can either stand up in your problem or sit down. Difficult times and situations are not meant to break you, break us, but if we let them, they will.

Isaiah 41:13–14 says, "I am the LORD your God; *I strengthen you and tell you, 'Do not be afraid; I will help you.'*" The LORD says, "The LORD says, "... *don't be afraid;* I will help you. I, the holy God of Israel, am the one who saves you," (Good News Translation, emphasis added). I hope you noticed that you were reminded twice to not be afraid, as God Himself will protect you.

Difficult times are inevitable. As long as you are alive, you will face trials. You can make surviving your situation inevitable as well.

I hope that the following passage from Success.com: *16 Rich Habits*, will help to motivate you to persevere away from fear:

> **Fear is perhaps the most important negative emotion to control.** Any change, even positive changes such as marriage or a promotion, can prompt feelings of fear. Wealthy people have conditioned their minds to overcome these thoughts, while those who struggle financially give in to fear and allow it to hold them back. **Whether you fear change, making mistakes, taking risks or simply failure, conquering these emotions is about leaning in just a little until you build up confidence.** It's amazing how much confidence helps. (Emphasis added.)

In difficult times, build your confidence to find the power to persevere. If you have to fake it, go ahead. Talk yourself up with positive words until you believe them. Change your thoughts as they control how you feel. If your thoughts are always on the negative, you will get negative results. Find the thoughts that are holding you back and evict them. It's time to organize your thoughts and persevere.

The coronavirus, or whatever you are facing, is just another thing to overcome.

The power is in YOU. Do not give your power away to fear or COVID-19.

Build resilience. Be intentional.

Start planning for the future–this too shall pass.

May the God of hope fill you with all joy and peace as you trust in him so that you may overflow with hope by the power of the Holy Spirit (Romans 15:13).

GOD SPECIALIZES

Have you any rivers
That seem uncrossable?
And have you any mountain
That you cannot tunnel through?

God specializes
In things thought impossible
And He will do what no other
No other power but holy power can do.

WHISPER HIS NAME[32]

Whisper His name
Whisper His name
Whisper His name
And He will answer you.

Whisper His name
Whisper His name
Whisper His name
And He will come to you.

Call out His name (Jesus)
Call out His name (Jesus)
Call out His name (Jesus)
And He will come to you.

Shout out His name (Jesus)
Shout out His name (Jesus)
Shout out His name (Jesus)
And He will run to you.

For when we lose our selfish pride
And when we fall down on our knees
For when we lift our hands
And say, "You're all I need."

---

[32] Whisper His Name, Johnathan Stockstill, Pastor, Deluge Band

Oh, God, we lose our selfish pride
Lord, we fall down on our knees
We lift our hands to You
And say, "You're all we need."

You're all we need
You're all we need
You're all we need

Glory to You in the highest place
Glory to You in the highest place
Glory to You in the highest place.